Spring Thunder:
Awaken the Hibernating Power
of Life

Spring Thunder:
Awaken the Hibernating Power of Life

by
Hua-Ching Ni

SEVEN STAR
COMMUNICATIONS
SANTA MONICA

The College of Tao offers teachings about health, spirituality and the Integral Way based on the teachings of Hua-Ching Ni. To obtain information about Mentors teaching in your area or country, or if you are intereted in teaching, please write the Universal Society of the Integral Way, PO Box 28993, Atlanta, GA 30358-0993 USA. To obtain information about the Integral Way of Life Correspondence Course, please write the College of Tao, PO Box 1222, El Prado, NM 87529 USA.

Acknowledgments: Thanks and appreciation to Suta Cahill and Janet DeCourtney for their assistance with this book. Cover design and photograph: Janet DeCourtney, John Rugis, and San Gee Tam, with assistance from Jim and Barbara West.

Published by:
Seven Star Communications Group Inc.
1314 Second Street
Santa Monica, CA 90401 USA

First Printing February 1996

Library of Congress Cataloging-in-Publication Data
Ni, Hua Ching.
   Spring thunder : awaken the hibernating power of life / by Hua-Ching Ni.
      p. cm.
   Includes index.
   ISBN 0-937064-77-7
   1. Meditation. 2. Spiritual life--Taoism. I. Title.
BL 627.N5 1996   95-49229
299'.51444--dc20   CIP

*Dedicated to those who know
that there are many ways of doing meditation
but there is only one way to achieve from it:
the natural and direct way.*

To all readers,

According to the teaching of the Universal Integral Way, male and female are equally important in the natural sphere. This fact is confirmed in the diagram of *T'ai Chi*. Thus, discrimination is not practiced in our tradition. All of my work is dedicated to both genders of the human race.

Wherever possible, constructions using masculine pronouns to represent both sexes are avoided. Where they occur, we ask your tolerance and spiritual understanding. We hope that you will take the essence of my teaching and overlook the limitations of language. Gender discrimination is inherent in English. Ancient Chinese pronouns do not differentiate gender. I wish that all of you will achieve yourselves well above the level of language and gender.

Thank you, H. C. Ni

Contents

The Universal Way

The Universal Way is the destination
of all spiritual efforts of humankind.
It serves all people's lives,
everywhere and always.

The Universal Way conveys the deep truth
of all conscious elaborations of the human mind.
It contains the vast and profound essence
of the human spirit.
Thus it transcends all religious teachings,
leaving them behind,
like the clothing of a bygone season.

The Universal Way is the goal of all sciences,
but is not locked at the level of the intellect.
It cuts through all wasteful skepticism
and inexhaustible searching.
Thus it surpasses all sciences,
leaving them behind
like historical relics of the past.

The Subtle Essence that is sought
by all sciences and all religions
transcends all attempts to reach it
by means of thought, belief or experiment.
The Universal Way leads directly to it
and guides you to reach it yourself
by uniting with the Integral Nature of the Universe.

The Universal Way is like the master key
to all doors leading to the inner room
of ultimate truth.
It is the master teaching of all teachings,
yet it relies on no religions and no experiments.
There is no need for intellectual or emotional detours
that cannot serve the lives of all people
everywhere and always.
Follow the Universal Way beyond all boundaries
to the heart and essence of natural life itself.

Preface

The natural calendar of ancient China was divided into twenty-four periods of climatic change that measured the year by the earth's rotation around the sun. The first period is called "Spring Begins." One month later, the climatic period called "Awake from Hibernation" occurs, which is around March 5 or 6 by the Western calendar. The exact date differs according to Leap Years. The first thunder of Springtime means it is time for all hibernating animals and insects to awaken. I wrote most of this book during the time of the spring thunder that awakens hibernating creatures, so I titled the book accordingly in the hope of awakening the spiritual energy of all people.

Hua-Ching Ni

March 14, 1993

Chapter 1

Time to Awaken

Master Ni's New Year Message for 1996

Dear friends,

Happy New Year. Let us make a resolution to do what can be done to create a better world through an individual and spiritually cooperative approach.

I
The Challenge of the Future

In the universe, time is not measured in human terms, but human beings look at the brief moment before them and see no further. By the world's timetable, the year 2000 of the Common Era will arrive in four years. At that time, or at any time, there could be a crisis, externally or internally, that would threaten human survival. If so, there may be a natural sign in the sky, such as a significant planetary alignment.

Past experience teaches us that if such a crisis happens, we cannot do anything external to stop it. However, you can make important internal changes that may help you outlive any natural or social changes. I sincerely suggest that you cultivate an attitude of renewal. If you learn the natural way of life, you may be able to overcome all obstacles and safely cross the threshold of the new millennium

~~~

It is important to reflect upon the condition and progress of human life. I have been saying this for some time. Now is the time for all governments to change their negative philosophies, policies and programs, particularly those which have been established by military force, such as communist regimes that serve a group of political rulers and impose an unnatural way of life on the common people. The same is also true of conventional religions that promote distorted fantasies for the purpose of gaining political or social power.

1

Self-change is something that leaders and people can both do. Spiritual cultivation can produce positive change and set the course for a new life. Natural calamity may be unavoidable, but meeting and welcoming external change is more practical than being afraid of it. Throughout the ages, there are prophecies and other indications that natural disasters and other calamities may happen. I ask you to consider them benevolent warnings and use them for self-improvement, whether or not such a calamity really occurs.

One individual, Nostradamus, based his prophecies on phenomena in the sky. Other prophets use the same or different methods. Eclipses of the sun and moon or changes in the black spots of the sun have always affected human emotions and psychology, as well as causing earthquakes and destructive storms. People who deny nature, however, do not know how to make use of such natural events to bring about constructive change in their lives. Denial does not equip anyone for survival. Why wait for signs in the sky before deciding that it is time for a change?

Nostradamus indicated that governments and religions are responsible for negativity in human society, and that a natural calamity must fall upon them. They both claim to be humanistic, but in reality their claims are merely a sugar-coating for their drive to acquire social power and control. I hope that people will be able to break away from the evil influence of these two ideologies and thus avoid any potential for crisis.

Before the negativity of governments and religions dies away, however, there is hope that a harmonious universal society will appear on earth to inspire a spiritual awakening deep in the hearts of people of universal conscience. Tao, the Integral Way, never ceases its work. It is the gentle, everlasting life and ageless confidence of all people of natural truth.

~~~

The conscious mind is, ultimately, the key element of life. It has the power to save the individual and to save the world. In this message I will discuss saving oneself and helping other people cross the threshold of the new

millennium. The New Year is a good time for meditation
and reflection on the meaning of life and on your connection
with nature. It is also a good time to review my book *The
Time is Now*.

II
A Centered, Balanced Culture

There is no divine nature beyond human nature.
The most balanced human nature
is no different than divine nature.
Divine nature is your own self-nature,
unspoiled by extraneous desires and fantasies.

Prime Minister Rabin of Israel was assassinated in 1995
by a group of people who thought that they were carrying
out the will of God, but once you start to play the game of
God's will towards other people, other people can also
fulfill the will of God towards you.

How can you talk about the will of God? Godly behavior
is good common sense, or understanding the big picture.
When people say they are following the will of God, it is
just a rationalization of their own ideas to gather
conventional support to justify their outrageous behavior.

During the Gulf War in 1992 in Kuwait, we saw Sadam
Hussein, the President of Iraq, praying to God on television to help him win the war. We also saw the President of
the United States praying to God to help the United States
win the war. Behavior must be monitored by one's own
conscience, not justified by making the subtle sphere of
nature responsible for one's actions. Religious culture is
nothing but story telling. A humanistic culture cherishes
and supports the lives of all people, regardless of race,
religion or political ideologies. People like a strong God
when they wish to accuse or destroy other people, and
they like a weak God when they wish to do something
that others don't approve. Most of the time, people put
God in the role of Santa Claus; their disearnest behavior
has no straight purpose.

The most important criterion for cultural development is the basic health of human nature itself. The value of spiritual leadership, modern technology, or anything else depends on how well it serves human health. Whatever does not serve health can be considered harmful to human nature.

People come and go, but the world remains and provides an important environment for people's growth generation after generation. People should support the health of the world instead of using their lives to make a mess of it and create trouble for others.

Religions may have helped society in the past, but when people become stuck in one way of expressing the unlimited, indescribable spiritual reality, they lose touch with the natural harmony of the universe. This does not help, it only hinders.

During the past 2,000 years, many people have died for the sake of a fantasy that was promoted to them rather than looking within themselves for their true nature. Some people say that the Dark Ages were the 5th through the 11th centuries, but many people still live in their own Dark Ages of religious fantasy rather than create a renaissance of spiritual clarity within themselves.

The direction of my work is cultural and spiritual. The spiritual education I have received enables me to communicate a healthy expression of human nature. Life is a group of activities, and productive activity is very useful. I appreciate all healthy activities that support life.

The Integral Way presents the achievement of healthy activity in all aspects of life. We like to use the words healthy and natural to indicate something beneficial, not suffocating. A healthy, natural life is not found in artificial sainthood or any other partial approach to life. A healthy, natural life depends on good activities that increase one's interest in life itself. The Integral Way values everyday life because it is holy and great, just as it is.

I have already given you the criterion of being healthy by being natural. As a responsible spiritual teacher, I would also like to give you the criteria for useful, effective spiritual practice so you will not be carried away by the cultural wrongdoings of any generation or any place. You can also use these criteria to measure cultural values.

III
The Unadorned, Truthful Heaven

For generations, people of natural spiritual development have described what Heaven is like. I accept Heaven as the spiritual attainment of an achieved human being, thus it is a high spiritual condition. It is also the deep natural reality of a world of light and the amassed revelation of achieved ones.

In Heaven, there is no religion, no government, and no powerful leader or authority. In Heaven, all beings are self-governed and orderly. They are not selfish or egotistical, nor do they insist on a particular way of doing things. Each life is supported by good natural energy and has no need to misuse or suppress others.

Each being in Heaven identifies with the great harmony of nature and accepts others as completely as it accepts itself. Although heavenly beings may live billions of light years from earth, they can be very close to people of corresponding or coherent energy. They have no worries, no taxes, and are not burdened by anyone. In Heaven there are no names or numbers, unlike worldly institutions.

Heaven is enjoyable because life is pure. There are no drugs or alcohol in the blood of heavenly lives; there is merely light circulating within each being. In Heaven, there is nothing called truth or goodness or beauty, because everything is true and good and beautiful. In the world, truth comes about because there is non-truth, fantasy and hype.

In Heaven, life is pure and natural, not conceptualized or hyped. People who rely on natural energy are part of nature. Worldly people are only indirectly related to nature through the veil of their own psychological and conceptual blockages.

In Heaven, there is peace and respect for natural order. Heaven expresses a healthy, constructive attitude. It has no mental institutions, unlike the world where sharpness, smartness, and intelligence create conflicts in which each individual clings to his or her tiny self or tribe. People make the world unlivable, and consciously or unconsciously turn their lives into a heap of ashes. This is why Heaven is so admired and cherished, and why people feel a spiritual pull to go to Heaven.

· Now I will describe heavenly beings. In Heaven, when a life comes into being, it is complete and has unlimited freedom. Heavenly beings are not jealous of one another, because all lives are good. No one spoils the lives of others, nor do they spoil their own lives by complaining about others. In short, there is no confrontation between self and others, because each "I" is in each of "you," and each "you" is in each "me," but at the same time, as a separate being, "I" am outside of "you" and "you" are outside of "me." Simply, you and I are Heaven. Heaven is the harmonious union of all beings and things.

Heavenly beings are usually indifferent about gender, race, or right and left. This would disappoint people who wish to sit on the right side of God; Heaven does not have different sides, or seats arranged by rank. Heavenly beings also do not particularly love or hate anything.

Compared to heavenly beings, humans are much sharper. Heavenly beings don't make trouble for themselves. The habit of creating trouble is valued by people, not Heaven. For generations, the troubles of the world could not be undone because the sharpness of each new generation always added something to them or made new troubles out of them. Human beings do not know how to undo their own negative creations.

The earliest people are said to have carried the genes of heavenly beings, but those genes changed when people no longer respected their natural health and began to indulge in self-deceptive activities, making social rank and religion into emotional melodramas. Any religion or spiritual teaching that is used incorrectly becomes a cultural cancer that consumes the normalcy of life.

Nature has the power to rescue itself. However, the human race can destroy itself by being spiritually unfit to learn from nature. This is why people should work on spiritual purification. The survivors of any calamity will be those who have preserved the original genes of Heaven within themselves and who have purified and restored themselves through spiritual self-cultivation. *T'ai chi chuan* exercise was developed by Master Tsan, San Fong who, by conservative estimates, lived 217 years. *T'ai chi* practice illustrates the universal principle of gentleness and connects your body, mind, and spirit. It is the best foundation for converting physical strength into *chi,* and eventually into *sen. T'ai chi* movement can be considered a spiritual practice or ritual. Whatever style of *t'ai chi* you learn, the basic principles are the same.

IV
The Spiritual Goal of the Universal Integral Way

The spiritual goal of the Universal Society of the Integral Way (USIW) is to assist the health of people and the health of the world. As a teacher of the Universal Integral Way in modern times, I have purified my teaching style and my work.

Because there are many types of Taoism in China, I do not want to participate in the competition. Taoism is a monastic style of life, but Tao is above all lifestyles. Lao Tzu's teaching has little to offer religious sects. My learning and training also have very little to do with them. As an individual, I have renounced all negative influences and disconnected from religious Taoism, but I have not forsaken the high truth of Tao.

I interpret Tao as the "Truth Above Oneself" and the "Truth Among Ourselves." In this, there is nothing to forsake. This is the guideline for what I choose to learn and practice. Tao or the Way is so vivid, but it may appear bland compared to all the "isms" in the world. Tao has no limits and fits no framework, thus it transcends the general religious approach.

The Integral Way cannot be narrowed down to one religion. It is the core of all religions.

There are two types of religion. One type is a social or external system, such as Christianity, Islam and Buddhism, that attempts to structure society. The other type of religion focuses on individual self-cultivation through various types of *chi kung* or *t'ai chi chuan*. It is more of an educational system, like internal Taoism, internal Zen Buddhism and the internal approach of esoteric Buddhism.

When we talk about governing externals, all reasonable advice or discipline can be accepted, but many ancient religions tended to disrespect the female and devalue sexual health. Sex can have a positive value in human life, although it is unreasonable to either overdo it or avoid it completely.

There is a middle, balanced way, which is what the Integral Way advocates. Spiritually, the best foundation of society is self-government. There is more information about this in my book *The Esoteric Tao Teh Ching*. In internal self-cultivation, there are only two main precepts: govern the mind and govern the *chi*. Terminology and minor rituals may vary among different traditions, but they still benefit the basics of life. You need enlightenment and you need to guide your *chi* to help your spiritual development. Existing teachings were developed from ancient techniques and practices. Among them, the standard is simplicity and effectiveness.

Both Zoroastrianism and Manichaeism are ways of interpreting *The Book of Changes*. They emphasize the duality of *yin* and *yang*, light and dark, good and evil, but they emphasize the aspect of confrontation by promoting only the light as divine. Lao Tzu's influence reached the Middle East in about the 6th century B.C.E. Ahuramazda, the God of Wisdom, is no one other than Lao Tzu. Christianity adopted the last judgement, doomsday and other points from Zoroastrianism and took them further.

Islam adopted Christianity and took it further. If we retrace these ideologies to the worship of light, we have reached their common origin.

You cannot ignore the value of the darkness when you are in the womb of your mother. Darkness means you are unable to see. All the trouble of the human world is caused by people who are unable to see, even in full light. Refusing to see the light, religion has set a bad example by keeping people under the darkness of its own self-interest. Religions darken people's minds by not openly telling them that the light of the mind and the light from their own lives are the things to worship rather than emotional traps of religious ritual and drama.

The three aspects of Brahman are the equivalent to the ancient Chinese division of Heaven, Earth and People. This trifold concept became the three bodies of Buddha, and the Trinity in Christianity. In Taoism, it became the *San Ching* (Three Purities). As Lao Tzu said, "The Way gives birth to one, one gives birth to two, two gives birth to three, three gives birth to all things." No one can insist on one world culture, even though the universe has only one spiritual nature. Different teachers were motivated to interpret the one nature of the universe differently.

Mahavira Jina's teachings were later integrated into an important sect that become very popular in Chinese Buddhism, the so called Pure Land Sect, which is nothing other than the worship of light. Does Tibetan Buddhism go beyond the worship of light? Surely not. The Pure Land Sect offered simple worship through prayer to Amitabha Buddha, the One of Boundless Light.

As one who deeply researches ancient culture, I believe that the world's cultural journey has taken a long detour. The root of all religions is the light of the sun and the light of mind. The mind, which is natural energy, produces different paintings of the same object. Nature is all-encompassing. God is nature, not something supernatural that is beyond nature. Religions are overly serious, stiff ways of interpreting nature in the past, present and future.

In order to help all people, I have chosen the term Universal Divine One to avoid conceptual distortions and divergences. Universal Divine Oneness is Tao. Tao simply means to adjust oneself to what is right. Tao therefore expresses itself through self-confidence and a natural, unobstructed life. The Integral Way recognizes the Universal Divine One as all gods and Buddhas. In other words, divine oneness replaces fragmenting names and partial descriptions that were established by ancient religions around the world. A unified spiritual culture is the Integral Way.

Tao is the Way. The Way is ageless. The Way is endless. The Way is easygoing. It is people who make life difficult. How can anyone forsake the Way? The Integral Way is the healthy aspect of all cultures and lifestyles.

The principles of a good healthy life are totally different from religious dogma or political cant. A complete life is the main focus of the teaching of the Integral Way.

You win the game of life, as I see it, by always being in the process of renewal. If a person's thoughts or emotions become permanently stuck in any "ism," that person is a "dead" individual. Likewise, people who are attached to one way of spiritual worship, one race, one country, one family, etc., are "dead." You may think that converting to something new is very serious, but I convert myself each day to become a better and more useful human being.

I was born early in this century, a century whose tail we are still holding. In this short span of a hundred years, people have experienced the benefits and disbenefits of their culture and of the world at large. In my teaching I have worked on exposing the bias of religions that have strong racial connotations. The Tao I live and teach is the essence of the universe. It originates from the world and is inspired by nature.

The goal of the Integral Way is to help people improve themselves so they can lead happy lives, it does not impose any self-serving cultural framework or institution on anyone. Set rituals, myths and terminologies are substitutes for the subtle energy network that spiritually connects all people.

If anyone is attached to the word "Taoism," or to any other "ism," it is simply a tool they need for the stage they are currently passing through. If nature gives people time to grow, so can I. I give my children, my students, and my friends time to learn what is good for them. Meanwhile, I keep teaching the Way. Not the old Way or the new Way, just the Way.

Jesus was the first to introduce the Way to the West, although his teaching has been restructured by the Christian church in an unnatural way that leads people to become dogmatic and think someone has to be special before they can possess all aspects of life's natural potential.

I don't disrespect or disregard any spiritual achievement or useful practice from the millions of years of natural human development. However, I consider certain things unimportant, like requiring a student to serve the teacher, kneeling when speaking to the teacher, and accepting the teacher as a perfect being. Those things are not fair or real. They are religious child's play.

On some occasions, people like to entitle land and relationships, such as making a woman carry one's name. Heavenly beings see this as a bad human habit. In truth, the most respectable individuals are those who are untitled and natural. It is they whom we should worship and serve. When you are young, having a title may seem distinguished, but taking pride in this can poison the naturalness of your life. The value of being untitled is to remain open to the great potential of nature rather than filling a specific, limited role.

People who bear a title must fulfill the function or duty prescribed by the title. They should use their title to carry out its function rather than to feed their ego. Some people call me Dr. Ni because that was my function when I worked in my clinic. Others call me Master Ni because I am an authority on spiritual subjects, but I discourage any sense of social rank.

Many friends are concerned that I have given up the title of Master at a time when the world needs the strength of a mast to bear the main sail and direct the ship. I have not given up the task of bearing the main sail, but I can do the job without a title, because of my own growth and conscience. You can still call me Master Ni, but in truth I remain untitled and unlimited.

I recommend that the guiding light of the Universal Society be Lao Tzu's *Tao Teh Ching*. If we can realize its teachings, titles are not important.

I wish we could eliminate the concepts of a mast or main sail, or master. The world is all people. A hero represents the old-fashioned model of social leadership. The real heroes who make good things happen are ordinary individuals. They are the real masters. On the old ships with big masts, the main power for the ship came from the sail, but when the wind didn't blow and the sail couldn't be used, there was a crew in the bottom of the ship who would row. I would like you to row your boat in the quiet, peaceful stream by moonlight, which is to say let your good mind fill the sail and carry the ship of your life to its destination.

My own ship sails on the Heavenly River, which is the Chinese name for our galaxy. The earth is my ship. Its destination is infinity. I have hinted at this in my book *The Uncharted Voyage*.

Because I am trustworthy as a spiritual student and teacher, I was entrusted with the important spiritual achievements of countless generations. Although I am trustworthy, I don't claim to be error-free. Life is a process of growing and learning, so my teaching does not require people to be error-free, either. However, they must have the courage to correct themselves when they do something wrong.

Being trustworthy means you don't abuse other people or yourself. You must teach the right things to the right people. This principle should be continued by all new teachers. The spiritual mission of all responsible individuals is "a better world with better people." The actual fulfillment of this mission must be carried out by individuals who clearly know that they cannot expect the world to be improved by someone else. Each person must find his or her own self-improvement. Through mutual understanding and great cooperation, a better world will become possible. Such a big task needs the work and cooperation of all individuals of high spiritual awareness.

V
The Universal Society of the Integral Way

Social benefits and problems are both created by a few individuals, not by the majority. The majority of people are the beneficiaries or victims of the activities of powerful individuals. There has been no exception to this for generations, but powerful individuals need to find the right direction for their good energy. Historically, they have applied it in wasteful directions or in serving their personal egos.

The world needs more people who live quietly and who don't have social ambition but who have a sense of social concern to help others. Such people are usually objective and thus know more about what is right. Social activists should accept these objective-minded people, who remain detached from society, as their advisers and teachers. If their gentle, subtle advice is ignored, the achievement of those who are active will be negligible or negative. The USIW seeks to combine the best of both. It offers the wisdom produced by the objective-minded individuals of all generations at a time when wisdom and action can jointly achieve the social goal of a healthy, harmonious and cooperative world.

In ancient times, the way to gain power was through military riots. One riot replaces another riot, and is in turn replaced by yet another riot. Thus, the means of social improvement creates even more trouble itself. Lao Tzu understood this and so did not advocate revolution or partisan disputes like those of the modern democratic system which seeks political benefit rather than doing what is really right or necessary.

Lao Tzu emphasized the individual value of a natural life. Society should be a place where people can help one another. His way of achieving a universal society was described in the *Tao Teh Ching*: promoting the natural virtue of life above any artificial dogma. To achieve such a society, he encouraged people to not be concerned that they are such a small group or that they work slowly, but to focus instead on causing no harm to others.

My observation of the 2500 years since Lao Tzu lived is that the gentle approach values smallness and slowness, but we have not yet achieved our social goal. I would interpret his essential teaching as "balance" and "effectiveness." These are what the members, mentors and friends of the USIW should use as their means, their principles and their motto. Improving oneself is the first priority, because a person who is standing on a sinking ship cannot save someone else who has fallen in the water. I respect the individual who can work on himself 50%, and work on the world 50%. If all people would do that, it would be great. If you are in good condition, you can offer yourself to the great goal of a harmonious universal society. What are you afraid of?

Because the task is so enormous, all people must support and share the burden. It needs all the helping hands in the world. In these last several years, the Universal Society of the Integral Way (USIW) has been organized by those who are inspired by nature and who reflect upon the problems of today's society in order to support the teaching of the Integral Way. They are new leaders and teachers who have discarded religious fantasies and are willing to work hard to restore the healthy nature of the world. Their teaching is a selfless universal service done in the spirit of harmony and cooperation.

The goal and purpose of the USIW is a better world and better people. We work to guide people to become good people who belong to themselves. We work to guide society to become good by itself. All individuals with deep understanding, impartiality, and great acceptance of minor differences work for and support the health and well-being of society.

In ancient times, it took a teacher a long time to find someone to whom he could entrust the practices he had achieved. He needed to pass them down to the right individual, but recognizing such an individual requires a lot of time and achievement. The search for such a student creates a little conflict within the teacher. When you help people, you need to be impartial and just, but you must also maintain certain requirements.

The USIW is organized to develop students who can receive useful spiritual practices so that those practices will not remain the secret of just a few individuals or one family, but such things need to be taught to the right people. All people define themselves as the "right people," but the USIW establishes safeguards for selecting the right individuals.

In the West, the word master implies authority, but in my tradition, this is not the case. The word "master" simply means someone whom others respect. A teacher is someone who knows the value of other people and who can be entrusted with spiritual treasures and attainments. This definition of a teacher describes the mentors. New volunteer teachers, leaders and supporters are called mentors instead of masters in order to avoid self-establishment, because no one actually has any authority other than the unlimitedness of the universal truth.

Mentors of the USIW offer selfless spiritual service. If they need to, they can charge for their work, as long as they are fair. I expect all mentors to be self-supporting from an independent source of income so that their teaching is never clouded by the pressures of economic necessity. I support, and the USIW certifies, mentors to follow an agreed-upon standard for fees. I have also outlined a unified discipline for all of them in order to avoid creating teachers and leaders who will only make more trouble for the world, like politicians, who work at the shallower level of worldly life. Spiritually developed individuals can work as world leaders, although the central focus of the Integral Way is to offer a universal spiritual education to all people.

The USIW sets standards and requirements for service and teaching. It has a Quality Assurance Group that provides a quality check on mentors. Every year, a mentor needs to renew his or her license as a safeguard against institutionalized downfall. When giving public service, people must have good intentions. However, a spiritual group such as the USIW must also safeguard the public security. Usually public security means protection from invaders, like an army, but I mean the public must also be protected from possible harm or downfall from spiritual teachers and leaders. This is why the mentors of the USIW have established and agree to follow certain ethical and moral requirements.

A person who has natural teacher or leader energy is an asset to human society. However, many spiritual teachers and political leaders who start their teachings or activities with lofty aims or catchy slogans change the reality of their program once they seize power. No one notices the change until trouble occurs. Because leaders or teachers are more powerful than other individuals, they must have discipline. Leaders are not exempt from the rules; they particularly need to set an example for others.

Conventional society, and modern society as a whole, lacks self-discipline. Many teachers and leaders have just wanted to be in charge of others, which creates turmoil that can last for generations.

The USIW corrects this bad trend by automatic discipline for its mentors (teachers). Members are only offered suggestions and advice, although I encourage them to exercise their best spiritual quality to help the world and render selfless spiritual service. No mentor should ever become a slave to his or her own ego and carry the self-defeating burden of egotistic ambition. The authority of a mentor lies in service and dedication to the well-being of the world, not in any title or position.

The problems of ego are obvious. If a person engages in leadership or teaching before his or her personality and spirituality have matured, he or she cannot guide others to be content with a good life and with nature, because their real focus is nothing other than an attempt to conquer and rule others.

~~~

To support the world in passing through this critical time, your prayer is helpful:

The Jade Pivot of the Universe

All Nine Heavens,
grant us the Divine Lightning
that illuminates the darkness of the human mind.

All Nine Heavens,
respond to our need for the Divine Thunder
that awakens the human conscience.

All Nine Heavens,
respond to our request for the Divine Radiance
that awakens the universal soul in each of us.

This invocation is traditionally used to help people who are possessed or whose minds are destructive. When they read or say this invocation, they can be helped and even delivered from all kinds of trouble. Many people truly feel benefitted from reciting this.

It is also beneficial in general to chant the name of the Universal Divine One and the Divine One of Universal Awakening, either silently or aloud.

You are welcome to copy this New Year message and share it with people you know.

You are welcome to learn spiritual self-cultivation from the Universal Integral Way.

You are welcome to become a sponsor of the USIW.

You are welcome to become an observer of the USIW. You are welcome to become a member of the USIW. You are welcome to become a leader and teacher of the USIW.

Chapter 2

The Leading Song

The spring thunder of the year 1993 awakened me to look at when and where I live. We live in a time when the human race no longer makes use of its long experience to face the crisis of common survival.

Most people know that religions cannot provide real salvation for the human race. They only add to the world's problems by the deep conflict and disharmony that accompany the prejudice and hostility they incite.

We might expect science to help, but it cannot take responsibility for world salvation for two reasons: the application of its achievements to military technology, and environmental damage. For example, when the ozone layer is destroyed, whether any life can survive or not is questionable. There is hardly any scientific creation that encompasses a complete vision of life. The disparate work of different sciences cannot be expected to bring the blessing of peaceful survival to all people.

Politics has no salvation to offer either. For example, the Russian people wasted 70 years in a fruitless experiment imposed by a small group of leaders. For the past 40 years, Chinese society has suffered profound cultural damage by attempting to build a new generation strong enough to compete with the West militarily. On the other hand, if the political system in North America is the model for the whole world, why is there random killing in its streets, in its schools, its restaurants, its parking lots and even its homes? Safety does not exist in any sphere of our society.

We might expect education to save the world, but the reality of our education system paints a dim picture of what the world will look like under its new masters. Our schools create an intellectual blindness that cannot save the world or individuals. They only create the specter of ignorant people who will continue to rule the world.

Commerce brings no salvation either. Irresponsible manufacturers pollute our environment, and aggressive marketing techniques pollute the healthy minds of people, pulling their focus away from a simple, natural life by filling them with the desire to spend.

To see and to know all of this does not take years of spiritual cultivation. Most people are aware that the institutions and establishments of modern society have a negative and unhealthy influence, but no individual or society can do much about it.

The teaching of the Integral Way represents my personal effort to awaken all individuals and all world leaders to their essential nature so that the natural health of the human race can be restored. This is the only goal I have; I can do nothing more and nothing less to help the world.

So far it seems that I am a modern *Don Quixote*[1] or like the old Chinese man who decided to move a mountain bucketful by bucketful.[2] However, I believe that a spiritual voice does cause a response in people's hearts, and that it is people who make up the world. I talk about subjects I know, in the hope of refreshing your own wisdom so that you can make a clear choice between survival and ruin and know which way to go.

As a student of the Way, I would like to offer a few verses to start this book. By reading through the whole book, you might find a reflection of your own true nature and be able to work from it to build a better modern world. It all starts with individuals.

As the Ageless Master said:

The vast universe has its own deep nature,
    which is expressed as the subtle law.
The nature of the universe is hard to define.
Reluctantly, we call it the Way.

---

[1] A Spanish story about an old man who imagined he was a knight saving a damsel and did battle with evil.

[2] An older Chinese man led his family to excavate Tai Shin mountain, because it blocked their way.

Those who respect nature will find their life,
because the Way is natural.

Nature is deep.
Its response is subtle.
People may not notice it,
but negligence will invite trouble, near or far.
It is wise to heed the subtle law.
Doing so will help you have a long and happy life.
Deep knowledge of the subtle law
can serve any individual
and the entire human race as well.
Deep knowledge of the subtle law
serves all aspects of all lives.

Difficulty occurs
whenever an extreme exists.
Trouble arises
from following a single narrow direction.

True wisdom is no wisdom;
to be wise is simply to harmonize with
the deepest sphere of life.
The nature of life is not external;
it can be found within all lives.

Shallow customs can carry people away.
Circumstances can cause them to become tense.
In conditions of shallow contention,
people lose sight of a true, good life
and throw it away
for something that is unreal.

Wisdom cannot be taught,
but it can be awakened
by facing overwhelming trouble
that has been self-created.

All trouble can be corrected
*   when one acts soon enough.*
Even on the verge of wiping out all life
*   a gentle voice can still be heard:*
"Stop, go back!"
By steadily reflecting on the universal subtle law,
*   all people can find self-contentment*
*   in a natural life.*

Chapter 3

The Ageless Teaching of Natural Truth

Given by Lao Tzu to Yen-Shi, the Pass-Officer
Developed by Hua-Ching Ni

Lao Tzu, it is said, was a person who manifested his being as one with the subtle origin of the universe, which has no beginning and no end, yet which subtly and gently continues in eternity. After having lived in society for a long time, Lao Tzu travelled westward toward the border. On his way west, he had to travel over the pass of Han-Ku. When Yen Shi, the pass officer and a naturally developed person, saw a violet aura appear in the east and move west in the sky, he knew that a great sage would pass by. Thus, he cleansed himself and fasted, and made other preparations to receive the sage as his honorable guest.

After his arrival, Lao Tzu granted Yen Shi's request and gave him his teaching, which was compiled in a book called the *Tao Teh Ching*. Later Yen Shi became a teacher himself, and his teaching was written down by his students in a book called the *Book of Ascending to the West*. This teaching of natural spiritual development which Yen Shi gave to his students is recorded here in the following passages. His esoteric teachings were passed down by the School of True Civilization.

1

This is what the ageless one told me:
The Way (as Tao) is nature.
Naturalness is its essence.
No other words can describe it.
Naturalness cannot be made
by artifice or forced.
It is just by being natural
that everything in the universe is brought forth.

If a person practices Tao in their life,
life bestows the power of naturalness upon them.
Naturalness can bring health, prosperity,
goodness, truth, beauty and holiness;
one has no need to force anything to happen.

23

If such things were made to happen,
*   they would be unnatural and untruthful,*
*   for they would be only imitations.*

2

The ageless one told me again:
One who knows Tao does not try to make something
*   be different from the way it is.*
The Way (of Tao) cannot be made
*   or planned deliberately.*
The one who "makes" Tao
*   creates a separation from the original union with Tao.*

One who does not know Tao
*   is always bothered with thinking and talking.*
Yet, if a person does not listen to words about Tao,
*   or if there is no one who explains the Way as Tao,*
*   then no one can know how it differs*
*   from the unnatural approach to life*
*   that has become habitual.*

Knowing Tao is similar
*   to having a deep knowledge of music.*
A skilled musician plays musical notes on a fiddle,
*   yet he cannot pass his achievement to another person*
*   who merely receives the oral explanation.*

3

The ageless one told me:
Tao is so profound and subtle;
*   thus, the knower does not know the truth.*
The one who deeply appreciates
*   the beauty of the musical note*
*   is aware at the same time*
*   that the beauty is absorbed by the listener's deep self.*
Thus, he cannot produce beauty
*   by any amount of hard work*
*   or make the beauty reoccur.*

Beauty is contained in one's complete nature.
The mind speaks of experience
    which is already past;
        only direct experience is able to catch beauty.
Such experience cannot be passed to anyone else.

4

The ageless one told me:
The life of Tao is carried by people.
Tao is illustrated by all the healthy normal lives
    in the human realm,
    and by the ancient developed ones
    who illustrated such high truth.
When they were here in the world for a while
    they rendered their best services and teachings
    through the model of their own lives
    without the need for special titles, codes or molds.
Everywhere they went, they left no name behind
    and nothing which people might use to
    fight over differences in understanding.
Since they gave non-conceptual teachings,
    there were no dead words to create prejudice
    among future generations.
Their lives were about accomplishing,
    not ending or finishing
    like the shallow force of worldly leaders.

5

The ageless one told me:
Chi (as Tao) is very subtle.
Its profundity is like the boundless abyss.
You may have heard of it,
    but your mind still may not comprehend it.
Why do you have such difficulty?
Because thought and language are only descriptions;
    only with your pure spirit
    can you attain union with Tao.

*Tao lives with the integral one's virtue
    which exists beyond written words or images.
Then your being merges with the natural life spirit.*

6

The ageless one told me:
Chi *(as Tao) will dwell with you.*
*Value what you have at hand,
    but do not stay with the vehicle
    and miss the destination.
The opportunity to unite with Tao
    will happen naturally,
    so keep yourself in constant natural normalcy.
You need nothing else to enlighten you.*

7

The ageless one told me:
*If you learn Tao through reading books,
    you must thoroughly understand the function
    and composition of words.
If you learn Tao through oral discussion and lecture,
    you must pay attention to the meaning of the words,
    which is more important than the skillful use of words.
If you are diligent and undiscouraged in your search
    beyond what is expressible,
    there will be hope for you to find Tao.*

8

The ageless one told me:
*If you are on the correct way of learning Tao,
    you do not establish any external standard
    to measure yourself.
The correct way is within you.
Do not take an incorrect approach,
    and the bad experience of mistakes
    will not be known to you.*

The natural correct way is called wu wei *(non-doing):*
   that means do not try to do what is good for you,
   just do not do what is bad for you.
You do not need to be good at prayers
   but you do need to guard good wishes
   from becoming selfish.
Quietly move in a healthy direction.
If you do not disturb your own spirit
   by treating it as something separate,
   you subtly receive the support
   of the wonderful deep sphere of life.

9

The ageless one told me:
If you learn Tao, there is no place
   you can go to be closer to it.
Yet there is a place in which you can deviate from it.

Tao is not longing for a match;
   Tao is self-content with what it is.
Tao is alone and has no match.
Tao is still happy and positive.

If you think something is right for you,
   it may be just right for you,
   but it is not Tao,
   it is a situation.

Tao is self-nature.
Tao is not the choice between right or wrong.
Tao is the Integral Truth that supports
   the normal organic health of everything.
Tao is not a creation.
Tao is natural reality.
Few people know it,
   yet all lives and all things rely on it.
Few can appreciate this subtle truth.

10

The ageless one told me:
With caution and by being careful you are on the Way.
With high sincerity, you embrace the Way.
The one who travels on the Way
*   does not expect exciting things*
*   but remains calm.*
When you attain Tao,
*   you shall meet the Way*
*   like the water of a river*
*   concourses with the water of the ocean.*

Quietly and without disturbance
*   one is with Tao.*
His mind returns to his own being.
His being embraces his integrity.
Not a single thing is allowed to enter his mind.
He becomes highly receptive.
Nothing in his surroundings
*   can pull him away from himself.*

11

The ageless one told me:
Tao is without form.
It is elusive and evasive,
*   but it exists.*
It is like a tree before it grows:
*   no root or branches or leaves*
*   can be seen.*
They are only seen
*   when a seed has integrated*
*   earth, water, air, warmth and light*
*   with the variation of the four seasons.*
Chi *is the original shapeless energy*
*   of the seed, root, branches and leaves.*
It is also the soil, water, air, warmth and light
*   and the variation of seasons.*
Chi *is what supports all lives.*

The convergence of chi *becomes different lives.*
Different tastes and different habits
    are created by different environments.

12

The ageless one told me:
Where does Tao come from?
It comes from its own nature.
It is the entirety of subtle energy.
From Tao, multiple things are born.
They are linked together through interdependence.
Things return from what has been ruined.
Things reappear from what has been extinguished.
Yin and yang and the five phases
    of mother nature's primal energy
    are the deep reality of all things and beings.

Things are formed and transformed
    from the subtle substance of Tao.
People who are undeveloped
    are unable to see the deep truth.
They make their lives complicated
    and difficult on the surface;
    they feel proud of their ignorance
    and their self-undermining lives.

13

The ageless one told me:
How do you know what is evil?
Evil is what you have an inclination toward.
How do you know what is foolish?
Foolishness is not examining an unexpected result.
People who do not have eyes of Tao
    hardly know the truth of life.
The world is an enormous container.
Inside and outside of the container
    is the subtle substance.
Many small containers fill up the big container.

It is said:
  there is a big container
  filled with all worlds.
The subtle substance fills all things.
It also envelops all things.

All numbers can be equal to zero.
Zero can be expressed by all numbers.
They are differently named,
  yet they share the same source.

What is right comes from what is wrong.
It is important to follow the right.
What is right cannot be found by arguing!

In verbal teaching,
  what should be respected
  are not the words
  but what they carry.
One must directly understand the meaning;
  arguments are only established by fools.
Books are words.
Tao is above words.
Tao is the source.
Knowledge is the dregs.

14

The ageless one told me:
All people like to pursue blessings;
  this is how trouble is sown.
All people try to please the body;
  this is how to destroy it.
The original baby-essence of life
  can only be nurtured by simplicity and naturalness.
It is formed from non-being.
The form is not everlasting.
Do not look for things that would spoil your senses.

Look for the way to make the form enduring.
This means: do not allow a desire to grow too big
    and cause the loss of balance.
Even in the love between parents and children,
    impartiality must be practiced.
Do not be judgmental or laugh at others.
Learn from the good.
Forgive the bad.

15

The ageless one told me:
What is good or evil
    comes from the same source
    yet they lead to good fortune and misfortune.
Right application leads to good fortune.
Wrong application leads to misfortune.
Application refers to the time, the object,
    the amount of strength, and so on.
This leads to how people plant
    and how they shall harvest.

Learning Tao is beyond the level of saying that
    what you sow, you shall also reap.
Learning Tao is seeing the correct application
    instead of trusting in external retribution.

The truthful way to cultivate Tao is to nurture your spirit.
The false way to cultivate Tao is to indulge your form.
Your true spirit knows Tao to be Tao.
You can live with your life,
    or you can deviate from your life.
 The subtle power of life can make your form fly.
    It can move mountains for you.
Your form shall be transformed into dirt.
There is no difference between your form
    and other people's forms.

What you desire,
  what your ears and eyes like,
  pleasant sounds and bright colors,
  can create a burden for your life.
What your nostrils and tongue like,
  sweet smells and good tastes, can be trouble.
Your body is the source of burdens;
  from it you know pain, itching, cold and warmth.
If your mind becomes the slave of form,
  you suffer from worry, vexation and trouble.
When you are chained to your form,
  you do not know that it is such trouble.
Observing from ancient times until now,
  no one can keep their form forever.
Even the ageless masters become white-headed.
Who does not become old?

While living in the world,
  you can give up the vulgar way
  by not adopting worldly standards.
In order to keep your original essence
  you must make a transition from the false form
  to the true form of everlasting life.
If you cannot preserve your subtle essence,
  what is the use of being honored with a high position?

By being inactive,
  your spirit receives peace.
If you could eliminate multiple desires,
  your life would stay complete.
You would be less active,
  and your being would be united.

Learning Tao is the bright way,
  but the saying of the ageless one
  should be learned first:

The one who teaches the Way among all people
  applies no discrimination
  between rich and poor, close or distant.
One who can realize the truth should be respected.
Spiritual learning is to learn not to lose
  the essence of one's life.

16

The ageless one told me:
Heaven, Earth, people and things
  all come from the same origin.
From the simple energy of the beginning of transformation,
  there is the subtle light, the subtle truth.
People who cannot see the truth
  are like people who look at a big river.
They see the murky water
  but not the rocks on the bottom.
People who live in the world and keep busy-minded
  do not know where they come from,
  and do not know where they will go.
By neglecting the old age coming so soon,
  they never have the opportunity
  to be with their true essence.
One who can see the essence knows
  that yin *is united with* yang,
  and yang *cannot be separated from* yin.
Positive goes with negative.
Normalcy goes with sub-normalcy.
This is the integral truth.

What is past has not yet arrived,
What has not yet arrived has already passed.
Everything that is in the present is past.
Nobody truly understands time;
  how can people decide what is life and what is death?
 The truth cannot be told;
  what can be told is not the truth.
Those who are dumb may carry the eloquence of life.

One may play good music to deaf people
and they may hear it clearly.
One may play good music to people with good hearing,
and they may hear nothing.
Talented people may have high intelligence,
but it is not intelligent
to dwell on insignificant details.
The heart cannot meet Tao
if it has left the origin,
so how can people know Tao?

17

The ageless one told me:
If you wish to learn the Way,
learn to be with the subtle origin of deep wisdom.
All other wisdom is not born by itself;
conditions bring about its birth.
All human behavior is conditioned.
Those who can be free from conditions
make correct choices.
This is how their fortune is made.

The one who is the same as Tao
is accepted by Tao.
The one who is the same as virtue
gains his own spiritual root.
Many people live their lives,
but they do not know life.
They mingle with all lives on the surface
and they suffer gain and loss,
but they never discover the truth behind life.
They are greedy for glory,
they are greedy for benefit,
they are greedy for wealth,
but they do not see their own foolishness.
They have ample anger,
but they have no way to settle their minds.

They learn, but they cannot find their true teacher
  to answer their questions.

18

The ageless one told me:
The Way is subtle; who can see it clearly?
From ancient times,
  only a few have known of it.
All people have experienced all events;
  few people know that all events are created by activity,
  and that people invite their own troubles
  by creating them.
My learning is to learn nothing.
You can be natural
  without going into the realm of self-confrontation.

Flowers come from the top of a tree.
The leaves and stems come from the trunk and branches.
The trunk and branches come from the root.
When you return to the origin
  of the great creation and transformation,
  you find the vitality of life.

19

The ageless one told me:
What the Way respects is nothing.
What virtue respects is kindness.
What is important in ritual is moderation.
What is important in giving help is taking no credit.
What is beneficial to your own life is to give.
What is important in having faith in life
  is to be with life, which is different
  from the sediments of sentiment.

In the culture of hypocrites,
  something is used to seduce something else.
When the virtue of people becomes thin,
  everything is made to look beautiful.

Leaders talk as fast as flying dragons,
*   but their real actions*
*   are as slow as the movements of a turtle.*
Natural virtue is ignored.
People do not respect the Way;
*   instead, they pursue vain glory.*
Money and glory
*   are like images in a mirror.*
You can see them,
*   but you cannot fulfill life by them.*
All echoes come from the void,
*   but the void does not grasp the echoes.*
A hypocritical culture is the reflection
*   of human beings' own ugliness.*
People have been perplexed
*   by their own reflections for a long time.*
Cultural bewilderment is passed down
*   from generation to generation.*
After the hypocritical culture developed,
*   people had more difficulty*
*   in finding true guidance.*
Human nature has become twisted,
*   by greed and vain glory.*
People have lost their constancy and uprightness.
They are like idiots
*   who can never recognize their own problems.*
They do not know that the abuse of fire
*   will burn them up.*

20

The Ageless One told me:
Tao comes with life.
Life includes all healthy functions.
These functions should be used correctly.
Overburdening life with too many desires
*   is like letting weeds overrun your crops.*

Your eyes serve you to see;
do not use them to stir your mind.
The tongue serves you to taste;
do not use it to serve the desire of the mind.
The nostrils are to circulate air;
do not use them for unnatural smelling.
Your breath is a vital function of the body
for the use of nurturing the body.
It should not be used differently.
Your longevity depends on good breathing.

People grow crops;
life has its four seasons.
Energy is what keeps you alive
and keeps death far away.
Energy keeps you strong.
Do not use it for war and troubles.
Do not use it for any evil purpose.
Although you are busy,
it is better not to rush after your desires,
for that speeds up your death.
One may live a life without evil intention,
and do things only according to natural instinct.
Yet the fulfillment of such natural instinct
must be agreeable to others.
This is how to conduct a natural life of harmony.

Where does trouble come from?
You may have overextended your natural instinct
and made it unnatural.
You may have become greedy for the enjoyment
of your personal form.
You may have ignored the feelings of others.
Do what does not stimulate resentment in people's minds
in order to avoid conflict
between yourself and the five elements.
The completeness of life will appear at the right second.

Nothing that is established can be kept for long.
Nothing under natural light ceases to change.
There is always a subtle light in the world
*   which is unknown to people,*
*   yet which enables you to see change.*
There is always an inner light
*   which enables you to see yourself.*

Life and death are not hard to know.
When you are awakened from sleep
*   if you wish for your life form not to fail your life spirit,*
*   then allow your life spirit to govern the life form.*

It is time for your life spirit
*   to return to life by stopping your own external quest.*
Remain indifferent to worldly interests.
Keep your mind centered with your spirit.
By this pure concentration,
*   you avoid the disturbance of unnecessary desires*
*   and allow no artificial idea to stir you.*

21

The ageless one told me:
One who does not pay attention to one's breath
*   is invited to many events.*
When events start, your freedom is lost.
You are commanded by events.
If your mind is associated with the external world,
*   danger comes from the inside out.*
Danger does not make your life enduring;
*   it prevents you from living*
*   the fullness of your natural life.*
Whoever enjoys fame
*   will be tempted by worldly honors.*
Because of greed, he invites trouble.
His disease is greed itself.

When people make greed a habit
    they slowly undermine the overall health of their life;
    this cannot be helped by acupuncture or herbs.

To turn your ambition back to your own life
    maintain a single direction in your life.
The sages do not admire what people have
    but what they achieve.
The sages use nothingness to govern
    the beingness of life.
Nothingness is the great natural potential
    that allows all good things to grow in their own way.

22

The ageless one told me:
There are many books that are called "holy."
Their teachings express grandness,
    but they are not the deep, subtle truth.
What has been said is equal to the whistling of the wind.
Numerous volumes have numerous empty words.

Those who grow too tall will fall.
Those who move too fast will be slowed down.
Those who overextend their prosperity will face setbacks.
Those who rise must sink.
The wise one restrains what is overextended,
    and does what does not require extension.
The wise one respects what cannot be talked about,
    and plunges his life in the direction
    of making nothing happen.
How can the wise one accomplish that?
Tao is self-content to be what it is.
It does not look for its match.
Tao is alone and has no match.
A single person knows the union of yin *and* yang
    within oneself.

If paired, the wise one is happy being paired;
   no rose on the other side of the fence
   is more beautiful
   than the one on your side of the fence.
To have many is not necessarily better
   than to have none or few of anything.

The most exalted truth is hard to know;
   the highest kindness is seldom appreciated by many.
The most righteous is rarely known.
The one who knows what cannot be known
   has understood the pivotal point of learning Tao.

Do not allow anything to occupy you.
All trouble can be eliminated
   when you project only in a healthy direction
   and restrain the pressure of desires.
You do not need to learn to fly.
The great Way is vast;
   there is nothing that is not included.
If you can understand that, then you know
   that to approach what is right,
   it is only necessary
   to refrain from doing wrong.

23

The ageless one told me:
The Way is deep.
All things of life come from Tao, from one.
If you understand that,
   you know that emptiness exists in fullness
   and truth exists in what is false.
If you cannot understand the paradox,
   simply do not distinguish one thing from another.

If you are interested only in pursuing
   what can be possessed and is solid,
   then you become sick.

Your trouble comes from possessiveness,
*   which creates suffering*
*   as you alternate between gain and loss.*
To learn Tao, to learn the Way,
*   first give up all types of desire.*
Do not let your mind keep wandering.
Keep yourself quiet,
*   and keep your mind unoccupied.*

To have the knowledge of numerous books
*   is not better than to return*
*   to the simple truth*
*   of your own life.*
Although many books may make sense,
*   they are far from the deep truth.*
What books hold is but a shallow emotion.
It is hard for people to hold what is definite:
*   when they say yes,*
*   the truth is no;*
*   when they say no,*
*   the truth is yes;*
*   so people keep fooling themselves.*

Decreasing your impulsiveness
*   is the learning of the Integral Truth.*
The true establishes the false.
The false establishes the true.
Blessing may bring misfortune.
Misfortune may bring blessing.
Experience is not of high value,
*   because it comes after the event.*
Foreknowledge has no need to be pursued.
You only need to learn the subtle law,
*   and live a life that is earnest, normal*
*   and constantly developing.*

24

The ageless one told me:
The void gives birth to the solid.
The substantial gives birth to the void.
Tao is the natural subtle law.
It gives birth to one,
    and one gives birth to all things.
All things share the same source:
    the subtle energy of the universe.

Though all people are one species,
    no one values the essence within their own life.
They wish to be rich and famous,
    therefore, they deviate from the origin of life.
People pursue fantasies,
    and this is how they miss the truth of life.
The origin is evasive
    but all things come from it.
The origin is also in me
    so I do not need to describe it.
By keeping quiet, the origin will be with me.

25

The ageless one told me:
I was born from nothing,
    and I shall settle down with nothing.
My spirit gives birth to me.
My mind kills my life.
The mind is my trouble.
If I do not have a mind,
    how do I know I have trouble?
When there is no idea stirring in my mind,
    I do not know myself.
When I know I have a self,
    it is because the mind has been applied.
When my mind is stimulated,
    I recognize myself.

It is but the convergence of conditions
    that creates the reaction of my mind.
The convergence of all energy
    creates the most desirable beauty.
By seeing all conditions as different unrelated realities,
    there is no real being to beauty
    and you know that real beauty does not exist.

When you see different energy such as blood and muscles,
    you know that there is no such thing as individuality.
My body is the vehicle of my spirit,
    it is the house of my spirit.
My spirit is the master of my life.
When my mind is calm,
    my spirit stays with me.
When my mind becomes impulsive,
    my spirit takes leave.
Therefore, the sage does not allow the mind to stay active,
    but causes the mind to return
    to the original source before birth.
Before people are born, there is nobody,
    no trouble and no desire.
The sage sees no individuality,
    but by keeping the spirits with one's life,
    Tao, the Way and virtue remain united.

26

The ageless one told me:
All the ancient developed ones followed nature.
Tao itself is nature.
If I force myself to become nature,
    it is not natural.
Why? Because I adopt a special idea
    that is other than life itself.

27

The ageless one told me:
The windpipe is empty inside
    and its function is not solid.
The one well versed in living the Way
    can be both empty and solid,
    being and non-being,
    square and round,
    big and small,
    long and short,
    wide and narrow
    at the same time.
Accept what people see you as
    and do not establish any argument.

The wise who live under Heaven are like windpipes,
    they have nothing to compete over
    because they hold nothing inside.
This is how virtue returns to oneself.
Improper desire is the root of trouble and harm.
The empty mind is achieved by having no improper desire.
To have no improper desire
    is as natural as the origin of Heaven and Earth.
Once you are with the root,
    you have no need to know the root.
Once you are with the origin,
    you have no need to search for the origin.

Changing the desire to be and to have
    into the desire to be natural and to have nature
    will truly help your life.
The one who is well versed in the Way
    and who has reached Tao
    sees no Heaven above his own being,
    no spirits inside him,
    no separation from life.
This is how to reach the Integral Truth.

In the beginning, people who learn the Way
    are interested in knowing the difference
    between Heaven and Earth, spirits and soul,
    and such things.
Those on the deep level of learning the Way
    are not interested in these differences.
They know the subtle truth
    that there are no differences.

28

The ageless one told me:
The one who observes the Way
    is like one who observes water.
He allows nature to flow.
Tao and Teh: the way and virtue,
    the way and its attribute,
    the substance and the function,
    come from the same origin.
The one who knows the deep quietude of Heaven and Earth
    and unites with the deep serenity of nature
    embraces the deep life of nature.
If you achieve a universal mind,
    you will know everything.
You will embody the Way which has no form.
One who overly values form applies false control;
    the mind that keeps contacting the surface of life
    runs after everything it desires but catches nothing.
The mind sends away what it dislikes,
    but nothing can be truly sent away.
The truth of life can be far away,
    but one still is able to know it.
The truth of life can be intimately close to you,
    but you may not be able to see it.
Therefore, truly achieved ones
    do not look, hear, talk or eat all day;
    they only know how to be with
    the subtle essence of life.

29

The ageless one told me:
When people see, they see nothing,
*   when people hear, they hear nothing,*
*   when people talk, they say nothing,*
*   when people eat, they eat nothing.*
By being indifferent, they do not establish preferences,
*   because by keeping quiet, serene and doing nothing,*
*   they return to themselves.*
They return to the stage before they were born,
*   when they did not have a body.*
They do nothing to nurture the body,
*   but their body's form is complete.*
The body is filled with heavenly and earthly energy,
*   so it can be enduring.*

30

The ageless one told me:
All people should have sympathy for others
*   but they should also have sympathy*
*   for their own foolishness.*
If they have sympathy for their own external lives,
*   is it not better for them to love their own spirits?*
He who loves his own spirits
*   would rather leave the spirits alone.*
In order to leave the spirits alone,
*   it is better to keep your mind quiet.*
By keeping your mind quiet,
*   your life spirit will stay with your body,*
*   and it will last a long time.*

31

The ageless one told me:
Spirits give birth to form.
Form shelters spirits.
A form without spirits cannot grow.
Spirits cannot be sheltered without form.

With the union of form and spirits,
 they give birth to and support each other.
Spirits always love life.
Life loves spirits.
What can be achieved by the mind
 is to give up self-proclaimed sageliness
 and worldly wisdom
 to return to know 'the nothing.'
That holds all healthy potential.

32

The ageless one told me:
A sage is always peaceful.
He is at peace with Heaven and Earth,
 and with all spirits.
Most people are at peace with what is unpeaceful;
 thus, they are not peaceful.
The subtle law decrees that:
 what is too full will be reduced,
 what is empty will be filled,
 what is strongest will be destroyed,
 what is weakest will be strengthened.
Reduce your thoughts,
 return to naivete,
 stop competing intellectually
 and return to the simple essence of the sages.
When the world is still alive,
 people can still draw support
 from the universal mother of their life.
If one loves the mother of life,
 the bodily life can last long.

33

The ageless one told me:
Keep your mind unoccupied.
This is how great creation starts.

When you keep your mind empty,
harmonious energy returns.
One who is good at nurturing the body
respects the body's nature
without going beyond the nature of life.
One who is good at preserving one's life being
does not reveal oneself.
Therefore, the best way to govern one's life
is to dissolve the self
and to become one with the kingdom of bodily life.
Although the mind is not particularly active,
the whole kingdom becomes prosperous.
People (vital energy) are not scattered,
but are strengthened.
If people knew the eternal truth of life,
they would live differently.
They would give up what causes harm
to their body, mind, spirit,
energy and sexual essence,
and would maintain their sexual essence,
enrich their energy and keep their spirits.
Most people seek enjoyment.
They constantly exhaust themselves,
and thus exhaust their lives.

34

The ageless one told me:
The universe is a big vessel:
empty, but productive.
It generates things in a gentle manner.
It has no need to know how things are born.
If you try to grasp Tao,
Tao leaves.
If you try to be close to Tao,
Tao retreats.

The ancient developed ones can be our models.
They did not trust their lives to kingly thrones.

They also did not trust their lives to the gods.
They also did not trust their lives to the things they owned,
    but always emptied their minds
    and filled their bodies with pure energy.
Once people are achieved,
    within their life they do not feel they have a life;
    within the mind they do not feel
    they have an active mind.
This is how to unify with the spirits.
This reaches the mystical source.
The person who can do this is one with the Way.

35

The ageless one told me:
Because the wise one does not think partially,
    no trouble is created by thoughts.
By constantly keeping to the void,
    doing nothing and keeping quiet,
    the wise one nurtures their form
    and becomes positive and creative.
One who twists one's nature
    by being greedy for what is precious under Heaven
    and trying to please one's own emotion
    falls prey to all kinds of temptations,
    and military adventures start up everywhere.
Life should not make people tired.
People are the root of the kingdom.
Once the people are tired,
    the kingdom is abolished.
Here, "kingdom" means the body
    and "people" mean spirits.

People who pursue things of no value or worth
    invite harm.
If one knows how to maintain unity with nature,
    everything is accomplished.
By practicing no mind,
    even gods can be subdued.

36

The ageless one told me:
My life depends on me,
*   not upon Heaven or Earth.*
I can practice not seeing, not hearing and not knowing;
*   by not letting my spirit wander outside of the body*
*   my life can be as enduring as the Way itself.*
Although I am much smaller than Heaven and Earth,
*   I have my portion of energy; that is my root.*
I do not learn from the people
*   who do good deeds for show,*
*   charity for fashion,*
*   kindness for praise,*
*   loyalty for favor,*
*   and politeness for grace.*
They invite things only in order
*   to benefit from them.*
The one who practices Tao
*   is always self-composed*
*   and remains disconnected from all attractions.*
He seeks no fame for worldly accomplishment,
*   and maintains his integral spirit*
*   without exhibiting his light.*

37

The ageless one told me:
War is the greatest calamity under Heaven.
It is not a great thing.
Whoever knows that life is precious
*   does not engage in war.*

The high leader who cherishes the subtle truth
*   stays simple,*
*   takes no pride in military strength,*
*   and does not engage in conquering other countries,*
*   so nothing can harm him.*

38

The ageless one told me:
The energy of the Way is gentle and soft.
Although the Way is meek and amiable,
    it envelops Heaven and Earth
    and penetrates all things.
Gentleness gives birth to strength.
Weakness gives birth to power.
Under Heaven, few people know the root of universal life.
The sage knows how to respect "nothing"
    as the source of life.
"Nothing" has its source in the "void."
The "void" has its source in Tao, the Way.
"Tao" has its source in nature itself.

39

The ageless one told me:
Why do people take their lives so lightly
    and finish their lives so soon?
People themselves make this happen.
It is not that Heaven and Earth destroy them
    or that the Gods harm them,
    it is because they have too much knowledge
    that is beyond their own control.
Thus they endanger themselves
    and enslave their bodies.
They keep giving birth to trouble
    and to laborious tasks;
    finally they destroy themselves.
The one who wishes to be long-enduring
    cuts off ill preference,
    gives up ill desire,
    and turns the mind and the will back
    to the basics of life.
Once form and spirit are united,
    life becomes long lasting.

40

The ageless one told me:
People live under Heaven.
Do not allow the world to make you ambitious.
When you have a kingdom,
*   do not allow your ambition to go wild*
*   with the strength of the kingdom.*
When you have a nation,
*   do not allow your mind to go wild*
*   with the expansion of the nation.*
When you live in a family,
*   do not allow your mind*
*   to be unnecessarily bothered by the family.*
Although the spirit is within the body,
*   do not allow it to be unnecessarily bothered*
*   by physical desire.*
Those who practice this are called people of Tao.

41

The ageless one told me:
Trouble comes as a surprise.
Trouble starts at the subtle level.
Good is born from bad.
Benefit is born from harm.
Big is born from small.
Difficulty is born from ease.
High is born from low.
Far is born from near.
External is born from internal.
Noble is born from ignoble.
Active is born from peace.
Prosperity is born from poverty.
Yang *is born from* yin.
Therefore, being and non-being give birth to each other;
*   nothing and something accomplish each other.*
The achieved ones know to return their being to non-being
*   and non-being to higher being.*

42

The ageless one told me:
Fish live in water,
  and water lives within fish.
People live in the Way;
  and the Way also lives within people.
When water evaporates,
  fish are finished.
When the Way vanishes,
  people die.

Thus, sages know to return
  to the subtle origin before they were born.
They give up luxuries and pride,
  and uproot their worries.
Because they do not slave for the body,
  their spirits stay with the body
  and the power of Heaven and Earth returns to them.
By doing nothing and by making nothing,
  the kingdom (bodily life) becomes strong,
  and the people (vital energy) become rich,
  maintaining the Way and following constancy
  in subtle union.

43

The ageless one told me:
One has one's own kingdom;
  its root must be deep.
Heaven (the sky) covers us.
Earth carries us.
People are supported by all things.
There is no need to keep gold, diamonds or rare things.
One who lives beyond Heaven and Earth
  can manage Heaven and Earth.
The one who lives beyond the bodily life
  can live long.
What most people think is good
  the achieved one may not think is good.

Achieved ones like what people do not like.
Achieved ones are happy about
*   what most people are unhappy about.*
They do what most people do not do.
They believe in what most people do not believe in.
They behave in a way that most people do not like to behave.
Their virtue is complete and
*   their way is complete.*

44

The ageless one told me:
The Way is not only with me,
*   but with all things.*
Because all things do not know to establish themselves,
*   they move along with the Way.*
All people receive life and gain the spirit,
*   but they do not know to value the spirit*
*   that supports their lives.*

The Way bestows its virtue on all people,
*   but people do not know they are supported*
*   by the virtue of the Way.*
Sages hide their spirits within their lives
*   so their spirits do not become scattered.*
Because they stay close to the mother, their lives are safe;
*   the people become strong,*
*   and the kingdom can be preserved.*
When subtle energy is strengthened,
*   physical life is lengthened.*
All people know that there are Heaven, Earth,
*   all matters and lives,*
*   but they do not know where these things come from.*
If people know how to trace life back to its subtle source
*   they can unite with the source.*

45

The ageless one told me:
The Way of governing physical life
*   is first to be with Heaven and Earth,*
*   staying quietly with the beginning of all lives.*
Sages understand the truth;
*   they blend their energy with their mind.*
This is how they stay alive.
Most people exalt passion, love, greed
*   and physical stimulation*
*   as the substance of life;*
*   thus, they miss life itself.*
These are two ways to manage one's life,
*   but the results will be different.*

46

The ageless one told me:
The Way and the Power,
*   Heaven and Earth,*
*   Water and Fire,*
*   things and lives,*
*   high mountains and deep waters,*
*   all have their position.*
The Way is but the void, the subtle energy,
*   and all things return to it.*

If one's life is not entrapped
*   by passions and preferences,*
*   the spirits return to universal virtue.*

The sky does not desire to be clear,
*   but is clear of itself.*
The earth does not desire to be solid,
*   but is solid of itself.*
Dampness does not wish to become water,
*   but returns to be water of itself.*
Dryness has no desire for fire,
*   but fire hides in dryness.*

All things are shown with form,
    but true forms cannot be seen.
High mountains, great oceans and vast lands
    are not created for all types of lives
    to come and to stay,
    but all lives and all things gather there.
The deep ocean has no desire for
    fish or other types of water creatures,
    but all water creatures live there.
If people can keep themselves empty and quiet,
    although they do not worship the Way,
    the Way will return to them.

47

The ageless one told me:
I do not particularly relate with good people.
I do not particularly relate with bad people.
I do not particularly relate with people
    who are loyal and faithful.
I do not particularly try to do good or bad,
    but I know one thing:
    when people accumulate good energy,
    good things come.
And when people accumulate bad energy,
    their life ends.
Sages keep the beginning of Heaven and Earth
    in their bosom where they stay close to
    the mother of Heaven and Earth.
This is the practice of the ageless ones.
It is not for my mind to know all.
It is not for me to judge if people are good or bad.
What I must do
    is accumulate the good spirit above individuality
    and become enlightened.
Heaven and the Way protect people who do good.

48

The ageless one told me:
My way is calm.
I do not allow my mind to become subnormally active,
*   thus I can return to the vital source.*
My vital source, being enhanced by the subtle origin,
*   makes my root deeper.*
My life becomes strong
*   and is supported by its unoccupied center.*
This is how I gather the essence of life.
Things have their infinite essence,
*   so nature expresses itself.*
Nature does not reject anyone.

I am an ageless one.
My spirit returns to the unnameable.
My form may stop,
*   and my being may be extinguished,*
*   yet my deep life is inexhaustible.*
The one thing I would like to tell all of you
*   is to keep to the origin.*
Wash away contamination
*   and discard disorderly motivations.*
Quiet your mind
*   and keep to oneness.*
Once all the dirt is cleansed,
*   then you will accomplish the pure life.*

Q: Master Ni, you have made your own translation of several
classics. I feel that I learned a great deal from the classics
themselves, but I feel that I benefit even more from reading
the questions and answers in your books, because I am often
on the same level as those people. Would you answer a foolish
question?

Master Ni: No question is foolish; you can feel free to ask
me. The answer might be foolish, but only if it is not useful.

Why do I say the answer is foolish? If my answer cannot help the one who is looking for an answer, then my answer is foolish. The answers I give in my books and teachings do not usually come from me; they come from the deep truth of nature and all lives. You might consider them the accumulated wisdom of all developed ones. I reflect on what is right or wrong, true or false, and through my own distillation, I produce the answer.

When I give an answer, I am responding to who I am talking to. Sometimes a person may not need such a careful answer, but I still give it, because I think of answering as a service. Asking questions is also a service to other people. Therefore, do not worry about the questions you have.

Q: Master Ni, I have gained a better understanding of the classics from your work, but what do you get out of them?

Master Ni: Recently I worked on the *Shi Shing Jing*, which in English is "Ascending to the West." This is the teaching of Yen Shi, who was the pass officer who spent time with the westward-traveling Lao Tzu and asked him to write down his teaching. I hope everyone will get as much out of this piece as I did.

The teaching of Lao Tzu contains the most ancient teachings, and I accept his teaching as my life guidance. It has truly helped me. Although my learning started early, a much deeper understanding came after my thirties, when I had experienced more of myself and the world. I never fully appreciated the philosophy of the ancient spiritually developed ones until I was 35 or 40, when I became serious about transforming my general approach to life to the approach of the ancient developed ones.

In general life, you learn to get what you want. It's as simple as that. This is how you are educated by your father and mother and anyone else. Although some parents have different attitudes, a child always likes to be different.

Your individual physical and mental foundation of makes

you primarily concerned with getting what you want. People are also imitative; they tend to follow the influence of their brothers, sisters and schoolmates, and as they grow up, they also learn from society and thus imitate the rest of the world.

Besides recognizing that the basic foundation of human life is "getting what you want," I think you would agree that there are not many people who can be called sages, or people of wisdom. Sages differ from most people by focusing on being considerate in getting what they want. Also, they are unable to give you whatever you want if it has an improper purpose or is unreasonable, unless there is a trade involved or a high moral notion is developed.

On most occasions, once you get what you want, you have accomplished your goal and you feel happy and think you are successful. If you are not lucky enough to get what you want in your life, if you are young, you think that you will get it next time. Surely your mind experiences setback or frustration, but you will find another opportunity. That is what life is all about.

Two types of attitude will be created by your life experience. One type is based on impulse. You do not believe in anything or adopt any philosophy; you just want to get what you want. If that is your approach, it becomes a kind of faith. When you cannot achieve your goal, you are still confident that you will get it next time, from somebody else.

The second attitude transforms this kind of desire or ambition into religious fervor, and you create an intermediary who can help you achieve what you want through prayer. When you cannot get something by depending on your father, mother, teacher or anyone else, you might create an imaginary psychological dependence, yet the fact that you still want to get what you want has not changed. So you invent God. At this stage, you do not know good from bad, you just want to have it. Thus, if you use religion to support the desire to get what you want, nothing deeper than assisting your desire.

One day you might experience that you can get whatever you want, but does it really benefit you? If you reflect upon your successes and failures, you might find that sometimes your failures are more beneficial than your successes, and sometimes your successes are unbeneficial. This is one step of growth, and now you can learn from the wise teachers. Most people have no chance to change this deep psychological attitude about getting what they want until their death. Even if they follow a religion, their religion only supports them in trying to get what they want. They never understand that getting what they want may poison them.

In my late 30's, I started to appreciate the teaching of Chuang Tzu. Before that, I thought he was negative, passive and cold, but after I understood him, I found him to be totally different. He is not cold, but refined. He is not impulsive, but reasonable. He is not negative, but deeply positive toward life. After studying Chuang Tzu and other books, I went back to Lao Tzu and found him to be even more broad than Chuang Tzu. Chuang Tzu emphasized spiritual freedom and advocated sometimes parting from the masses. Lao Tzu had great sympathy for the masses. Although he retreated from general society, he did what he could: he left a book. My appreciation for Lao Tzu is still greater than for Chuang Tzu, yet Chuang Tzu was a great help to me in my 30's and 40's.

How did I change before my 30's? In my youth, I wished to be distinguished, to be somebody special, have special achievement and receive special treatment in all things. For example, if I went to see a Chinese opera, I had to sit in the best seat. After studying Lao Tzu and Chuang Tzu, I became content with being undistinguished.

When I was young, I liked to be stylish in my manners and clothes. I hoped that people would treat me the same, and they did, but I never had a true friend, because everything was superficial. Still, deep in my heart, I liked to get what I wanted, but after I deeply understood Lao Tzu and Chuang Tzu, I gave up my desire to be stylish and I learned to be original. I learned to laugh, to be angry freely without overdoing it. From artificial, I became original.

Also when I was young, I liked things to be grand, complex, and perfect in all respects, including my own learning, work, life attitudes, social position, etc. Then after learning Lao Tzu and Chuang Tzu, I suddenly discovered that being simple was truly more beneficial and enjoyable than being complicated or lofty. When I came back to this, my friends, especially my past close friends, all said that I had changed. I asked them, do you love me better now than before? They could not say, but slowly I understood the change. Before, I wished to be or do something that would please people; then, I wished only to be my real self. If people enjoy my company, they are welcome, and if they do not, I don't feel disappointed or think I am not good enough. At least I am real. To all friends, whether they are old ones, close ones or new ones, I am honest and natural. Sometimes I am appreciated, sometimes not, but I am trusted to be what I am.

At that time, I received many students. They became my students, not just friends any more. They really understood the value I set on being truthful rather than just distinguished, stylish, and so forth. My example awakened them to see where they had deviated and to appreciate what they really were. Out of respect, they moved from the friend level to become my students. I received support for the most part, but I also experienced some trouble from people who had not reached that stage yet.

To go deeper, you might ask, do you ever have psychological or emotional difficulties? Do you ever feel the need to be supported? Surely I do, but do I want to pray to god or go to temples for help? I do not, because what a temple or a concept of God offers is merely psychological help. I do rely on one thing only: the power of nature. If, for example, a person who has an internal problem, like a liver problem, vigorously prays to God to help him get out of the trouble, he would probably get more realistic results if he slowed down and looked for reasonable help; if not from western healing methods, then from eastern. The basic thing is to slow yourself down. Do not get excited or call your mom or dad or Heaven or anyone else for help. For most things, it is not God who can take care of your problem, but nature. Nature can help you if you allow it to perform its natural healing power. It is important, on occasions which you cannot do anything about, not to interfere with the natural, organic power of life itself.

All people have a mind, and the mind likes to take control. Most people think, "I must control everything: my work, my business, my family, my children, everything." That attempt at control is the first evil in life. The second evil is interference; people like to interfere if they have an opportunity.

The *Tao Teh Ching* teaches us about the evils of violence and aggression, but I am talking about the two evils of "control" and "interfere." In your life, you can control nothing. You can only work and build a good foundation, and then let a thing happen by itself. Building a good foundation for success is not the same as interfering. With more interference and more control, things do not happen as naturally, as well or as healthily. Things will die.

In Western culture, industry has conditioned people to trust "control." In addition, the commercial world has instilled the pattern of competition in people's minds. Too much control and evil-natured competition are both unnatural. You might ask me, how can you run a business or a society without control? Well, your body is an industrial manufacturer; do you manage your heartbeat or your breath? We wish to be in control, but these things cannot be watched constantly. As we learn the deep truth, we should build a good foundation that will allow good results to happen. Effectiveness is not synonymous with minute-by-minute control. Managers apply a good foundation with good rules, but not too much control. This brings about healthy growth in factories, in the market, and in the government and society.

When you strongly want something, like expecting a

relationship to last forever, that is unnatural, because nothing lasts thing forever. If I could, I would not have left my loving mother and father. I would never let them go away. I would pull them back to support me like they did when I was a teenager living upstairs in their house. They provided books for me, and with everything I needed to learn and to enjoy. I had no worries about the world. Unfortunately, I left home early. It was not that they did not like to provide for me, but there was a war. It was difficult to accept that, but it is impossible to return to the past. Follow the natural principle of having live, growing, healthy relationships. Do not expect even an excellent relationship to last forever. Just be natural. All people should take care of their families in a natural, healthy way without trying to control loved ones for selfish reasons. My parents did not. I do not.

You need to learn to treat the world calmly, whether it is good or bad, and to allow nature the chance to correct itself. Sages only teach people. They do not make the world do what they like.

The highest law is the naturalness of nature itself. Beauty, truth, goodness, and holiness are all variable; you should remain calm and self-composed, allowing things to change or not change without interfering. I live that way and am productive, helpful and able to enjoy what nature offers me.

In learning the Way, there are misunderstandings that can lead people astray. To help you, I would like to make a list of things that are easily misunderstood or misapplied. Once you make these errors, even by a hair's breadth, the result is as great as the distance between Heaven and Earth.

Be natural but not disorderly,
  original but not wild,
  organic but not ungrowing,
  normal but not stagnant,
  undistinguished but not sloppy,
  simple but not ineffective,

nonviolent but steadily progressing,
non-aggressive but achieving with agreeable effort,
non-controlling but building a suitable foundation
*   for positive achievement,*
non-interfering
*   but offering correct care and useful concern.*

Because I do not apply control, as some religions do, you may consider this a weak path. You may think it is useless because it cannot help you take advantage of other people. Why do you need to control or be controlled by other people? You can see from the past three thousands years, most people struggle for control and interference in the lives of other people. This is how society lost its original health.

If I could do anything for the world, I would just point this out and let people reflect upon it. I would not promote a powerful image instead of the universal divinity who is the subtle law of everything. Nature can help you dissolve all trouble without making you psychologically dependent. Reason should replace the control tactics of the Roman Empire or the Catholic Church or many of the Chinese dynasties.

The only truth is the ageless truth, that is Tao. This time-tested truth is appreciated by everyone who has attained growth. How you live is your personal choice. You can choose leaders and religions that take advantage of people, or you can choose to make a change for a better, healthier society.

Chapter 4

Natural Meditation

Natural Meditation is For Those of Spiritual Self-Accomplishment

I

Although I have given the general instruction for doing Natural Meditation, in my book *The Gate to Infinity: Realizing Your Ultimate Potential*, you may wish to know more about it.

Natural Meditation can be helpful to almost everyone's spiritual achievement. Let me tell you how to start meditation. I suggest that you do some preparatory physical movement before you meditate, and some adjusting movements after it. If you have learned Eight Treasures or *Dao-In*, you can adopt some movements from both systems before and after meditating. The purpose of doing movement before meditation is to change your energy flow to become thinner inwardly. Afterwards, gentle movement will restore the general condition of your energy so you can adapt to life activity again.

The correct postures for meditation are illustrated in the *Workbook for Spiritual Development of All People* and in the second part of *Attune Your Body With Dao-In*. Whatever posture you choose, it is better to continue using one of them until it gives you some positive result rather than change postures too often. Changing too often disturbs the serenity, quietude, stillness and stability that help transform the quality of your energy.

If you are a beginner, or if you have a minor emotional disturbance, you can use any meaningful invocation or sounds. However, if you overuse an invocation, especially one that consists primarily of sound vibrations, its sedating effect can cause your body to function unnaturally. If you wish to use an invocation with a clear meaning, you still need to select the correct one for your need. However, all such things are introductory, auxiliary activities. Knowing how to use them is an art and a skill. If you are direct and determined to go forward to unite with the subtle universal essence, you may not choose to practice the invocations.

If you do not do anything special, in the beginning minutes of your meditation you still need to practice a type of physical self-inspection. Make certain you are sitting upright and comfortably, and check whether your clothes are too tight. If you have any pain or pressure in some spot, then adjust it. Then inspect your emotions to see whether there is any irritation, anger, fear, etc., so that you can adjust them to be balanced and harmonious. Then examine your psychology to find out whether there are any unrestrained thoughts or motives in your mind; if there are, undo them. Once you have done all that, and everything is normal and peaceful, then gather yourself to concentrate on nothingness like the full moon or zero ("O") and establish a marriage between your life being and the pure form. The pure form is the true, non-material form of your subtle life.

The purpose of spiritual cultivation is to unite the physical form with the subtle essence. In general, the subtle essence is elusive because people are not masters of themselves. Self-mastery can only be experienced and attained through serenity. With dissolution, you are unaware of both the physical form and the pure form. Meditation is good training for learning the serenity of deep being. This is the purpose and practice of Natural Meditation.

Here are some things to remember in your practice:

Too much movement is a deviation.

Too much technique is also unbeneficial as it obstructs the pure purpose of natural meditation.

The purpose of natural meditation is to nurture the universal or immortal personality described in *Stepping Stones for Spiritual Success*.

When undertaking quiet sitting in meditation, gentle concentration on the energy transformation from coarse to refined and pure will naturally take place.

Mental sublimation from intellectual struggles to the attunement of natural wisdom is the natural outcome of effortless, natural meditation.

Q: Master Ni, esoteric Buddhism incorporates many types of visualization, and different schools of Taoism emphasize orbit circulation. Can I practice natural meditation without doing anything else?

Master Ni: Various methods of visualization are designed to allure beginners who have no spiritual knowledge of their own. This is a device, not an achievement. Orbit circulation can only be experienced when one engages in quiet sitting. Good concentration produces good results. Small techniques create confusion.

Various techniques are similar to different sects of churches or religions. Can a different spiritual reality be reached? There is only one spiritual reality: the universal spiritual nature of life.

Once a master of Buddhism attained enlightenment and sang the following poem:

By looking for Buddha in the outside world,
    you find only emptiness.

By looking for Buddha inside my being,
    you find none.

Here is my own advice after many years of painstaking meditation.

If you learn to open your heart
    as wide as the universal valley,
You will find that all religious truth
    is right in the center.

Q: In some traditions, when you sit in meditation, you are supposed to strive for samadhi *or* nirvana. *Is that a correct goal?*

Master Ni: If you meditate to escape the pain of life, you will only attain numbness of mind, which is fruitless. Such meditation establishes duality: one side of the mind commands the other to be quiet. Then the other side tells the first one to be quiet, like children playing seesaw in a playground. In that way, you just keep playing seesaw in the playground and you go nowhere.

True practice does not support one side or the other. With detachment, you can attain unification between the self and non-self. You can also attain unification between the mind and body naturally, effortlessly and beautifully.

In doing Natural Meditation, you pursue nothing, you simply allow the natural condition of your being to maintain its own organic creativity. Here you might apply the term *wu wei*, which means to make no willful interference in the wholeness of the mind.

Q: Is this achievement?

Master Ni: Your achievement is natural. Nature brings about the world. Nature brings about a healthy attitude toward life. You do not need any gimmicks. You only need to sit well and not pursue impulsive desires that turn into imaginative fantasies. By doing nothing, you will safely reach the infinite ocean of wisdom.

Q: Is meditation all-able?

Master Ni: No, not at all. I trust rhythmic life.

Q: Master Ni, what is a rhythmic life?

Master Ni: *Having time to rise,*
    and time to lie down.
Having time to sit quietly
    and time to stretch freely.
Having time to stand still,
    and time to move around.
There is time for meditation
    and time for stretching.

It is what Lao Tzu calls "wu wei,"
which means to do nothing
against the deep nature of great life.
Let nature be your life.

In stillness,
there is movement.
In movement,
there is stillness.
If one knows this,
one will not be partial to one way or another.
While you are alive,
enjoy all postures.
They are equally holy
as manifestations
of the Universal Divine One.

Q: Why do some teachers say they would like to sit in meditation for their whole life?

Master Ni: What they tell you depends upon what they sell. I need to warn you that prolonged meditation is not as helpful as short, effective meditation. At different ages and in different environments, standing meditation is sometimes more helpful. This is described in the *Workbook for Spiritual Development of All People.* Moving meditation such as the practice of *chi kung (chi gong)*, Eight Treasures, Unity/Trinity *T'ai Chi* Movement, Gentle Path *T'ai Chi* Movement, etc., is also helpful. All practices assist you to develop as a complete human being.

Meditation is not a comatose state of being, but neither is it an opportunity to sit and think about your emotions or troubles or fantasize over the fruits of your labors.

Q: Master Ni, if life itself is natural, then why meditate?

Master Ni: That is a good question. Being natural usually means that you do not need to do anything extra.

Fundamentally, each life is a small model of nature. We learn from and also receive support from the big model. Some people are able to learn the subtle laws from the big model in order to guide the small models of their own lives to be more natural. Because they do nothing against nature, they are still natural. Because Natural Meditation is the learning of deep nature, it does not go against nature. Meditation only becomes unnatural when you think of it as the only worthwhile thing to do in life. For example, anyone who retreats to a cave or somewhere else to do full-time meditation will find that such practice is not really beneficial.

Q: Master Ni, you mentioned that each human life is a small model of nature, and that we can learn from nature. How and what can we learn from nature?

Master Ni: If your question focuses on meditation, then my answer will not be stretched so widely that you cannot catch my point. Many small techniques, thousands of mantras and hundreds of different visualizations have been developed for meditation. These may have been designed to help you become a Buddha or a holy being, etc. Being natural is totally different from using small techniques from books or buying them from a special teacher.

So far, human life has been bound to earth, thus earthly life is the foundation that we have experienced for millions of years. The energy of human life comes from the sun, moon, Big Dipper and 28 constellations. Most people understand that human beings are formed by nature, but after we are born, we are still being shaped by nature, supported by the food we eat and shaped by society. The formation and transformation of life keeps going on and never stops. Therefore, if we learn about nature, we can also attain a certain amount of self-mastery and reduce the physical pressure of nature and society. Learning about nature means harmonizing with nature or reducing its negative influence.

Q: I would like to know how to do this.

Master Ni: It is not a matter of how, but of personal growth. First you learn how the day is divided. Most people use daylight to divide day and night. Ordinary people generally start their day around 6:00 a.m. and finish their day around 6:00 or 7:00 in the evening. Usually, they stay awake until 10:00 or 11:00 p.m.

For people who are serious about spiritual cultivation or meditation, the day is different. Their day starts at about 11:00 p.m. or midnight and is finished at noon or 1:00 p.m. The night cycle goes from 1:00 to 11:00 p.m. In meditation, the life force comes from the sun, directly or indirectly. Sometimes we call the sun *"yang* energy"; actually, it is life energy. If you do not have life energy, your life will wither, just like the lives of flowers, which also need direct or indirect light. Although totally dark places have some forms of life, vegetation will usually turn toward any direction that has light.

The natural energy of human life follows the solar energy cycle. Spiritual life also follows the solar cycle.

Now I will give you some basic principles that can help you understand what needs to be done and what is an appropriate hour for meditation, if you are interested in knowing that.

Q: Yes, I am.

Master Ni: After midnight, the upward cycle starts and the energy in our body rises from the soles of the feet. This continues until noon, when the energy reaches the top of the head. This part of the day is called "advancing *yang* energy," which in energy terms is *called "Jing Yang Fo."* *Jing* means increasing, *yang* means sun or energy, *fo* means fire; together, those words mean the generating energy is rising.

The cycle from noon to midnight is called "Retreating *Yang* Energy." The ancient naturally developed ones called this "*Tui Yin Fu.*" *Tui* means regressing, *yin* means the opposite of *yang*, and *fu* means to be in accordance with nature. Beginning at noon, the *yang* energy in the body retreats from the top of the head and starts to sink to the feet.

"Advancing *yang* energy" also refers to cultivation with motion or vigorous breathing, which pumps the energy upward in the body. It is suitable to do this in the upward cycle of a day, i.e. from midnight to noon or in the morning. "Retreating *yang* energy" also refers to peaceful or motionless practice or gentle breathing that reduces *yang* energy. It is suitable to do this during the downward cycle, i.e., from afternoon to midnight.

No matter where you live, the cycle from midnight to noon is beneficial for meditation that increases your *yang* energy, in other words, your normal, healthy vital force. This is how to ride the solar cycle of natural energy in the body; there is no need for artificial effort.

If you meditate at midnight, it means you are meditating during the transition when *yin* energy reaches its peak and naturally switches to the *yang* cycle. That energy hour (the two hours between 11:00 p.m. and 1:00 a.m.) is the transition hour from *yin* to *yang*. If you meditate from five minutes to one hour at that time, you receive five pluses. That is the best hour for meditation.

When I was younger, for a period of 15 years, there was no bed in my bedroom but only my meditation equipment, a small cushion. Most of the time I slept sitting up, so there was no distinction between my meditation and my sleep.

Before that, I did a standing position as my main practice, combined with sitting meditation and walking meditation. I also taught movement as a career for ten years. Now, I live a regular life, but in the morning time it is necessary to attune myself and adjust my energies after a night's sleep. I need a whole night's sleep, because I have so much physical activity. There is a traditionally valued principle of not exhausting yourself with any of the practices, but allowing growth to occur naturally. Most of my life, I have enjoyed a free and inspiring lifestyle whenever I could.

For the most part, I do what I recommend here, which is dynamic Natural Meditation with various postures. Sitting meditation is always balanced with standing meditation, walking meditation and sleeping meditation, plus constructive activities that support my life. I teach mostly as a service.

People who go to sleep late, such as after midnight, might think that the hours around midnight are a good time for them to do meditation. However, because they are active at night, meditation is not really their central practice. If you do midnight meditation, you have to prepare by going to sleep early so that you are rested and have better concentration. This schedule is not based on modern life with electric lights that blur the difference between day and night.

In ancient times, as soon as it got dark, you had to go to sleep. Then at midnight, when the *yang* energy began to rise, men and women became restless, but spiritual people used that hour for meditation.

If you do a lot of strenuous work in the daytime, I suggest that you sleep soundly. The next morning, you can meditate before 6:00 or 7:00 a.m., and if you are an early riser, around 2:00 or 3:00 a.m.. If you meditate any time in the early morning, you still earn three pluses, energywise. Because the energy is so subtle, there is no way to really discuss it, so I use a system of pluses so you will know which times are better.

If you meditate before 10:00 a.m. or noon, you still receive one plus. Noontime receives zero. In the afternoon, when *yang* energy is declining, you actually receive a minus.

Q: So it is not good to meditate in the afternoon?

Master Ni: It is okay for certain purposes. People who have a troubled mind can do so, but this kind of meditation is not for increasing energy. If you are too mental, any help is welcome.

Second, people who have high blood pressure or congestion problems, or people who feel too full of energy or whose energy is too strong and who might otherwise have a stroke will find meditating in the afternoon or evening more suitable.

The hours between 4 and 6 p.m. are beneficial for physical movement, particularly for people who like to exercise. At this time, the body is more able to reach its top condition physically.

In modern times, the hours of one's day are usually sold to someone else in exchange for money to support one's life, so there is only the evening and night for personal activity. That is because you are accommodating society's schedule. Many people take evening classes in *chi kung* or *t'ai chi* or *yoga*, but that is not ideal. However, for modern people, it is better to learn at night than to not learn at all. It is a good way to consume the heat inside of your body. Then, after you learn how to do it, you can practice your exercise at a better hour which you have chosen for yourself. If you do not use up the body's heat during the day, activity is required at night; otherwise, you might have trouble sleeping or you might burden yourself by becoming too fat.

People should not overeat, oversleep, or exhaust themselves having fun. This is also part of meditating, but even if you do not meditate, you will be naturally healthy and live long if you accept this advice.

When you meditate, whether you sit in a chair, sit crosslegged or do standing meditation, the single most important requirement is that your spine must be straight. All benefits can be produced by sitting up straight. There is nothing else of importance that needs to be emphasized.

In the orbit circulation, the school of internal medicine regards the section from the tip of the tailbone to the top of the head as the line of upward movement or "advancing *yang* energy" and the section from the forehead to the lower body as the downward direction in the front of the body or "Retreating *yang* energy." The inhalation of the breath is called "advancing *yang* energy" and the exhale is "retreating *yang* energy."

Intention may be applied to move the internal energy and combine it with the breath in order to create an automatic circulation of the energy. As a matter of fact, constant repetitions of strong inhalations will cause a person to feel warm, and continuously paying attention to long exhalation will cause cooling. This can help control the body's temperature.

If you are weak, pay attention to your inhalation if you wish to increase your energy, the *yang* fire. If you are a person who has blood congestion or high blood pressure, then use the technique of focusing on long, gentle exhalations to reduce your pressure. To control the body's heat is an art. In ancient times, spiritual people did not wear more clothing in winter than they did in summer, because they knew how to control their body heat. In modern times, this is not a necessary achievement.

These principles can help you understand the meaning of the terms "advancing *yang* energy" and "retreating *yang* energy," to make a suitable adjustment in your sitting. When you have attuned your body's energy condition, then you can gather yourself in complete transcendence so that the purity of your life substance is above all disturbance. After achieving this for a period of time, no matter how long, be sure to restore your normal condition before you engage in general life activity again.

Q: Master Ni, I have heard that sometimes spontaneous movements happen during a person's meditation. Is that true?

Master Ni: That is true, but do not look for it. When people who are physically active use their mind to discipline their body to sit up straight and not move, the body sometimes tries to rebel and shakes terribly. This is not done intentionally, but is a reflex of the nervous system. If your thoughts are not influenced by a religion that says that

God or the devil has come, then you are safe. Just allow it to happen and to slow down by itself. It will stop. If it does not stop, it is due to mental tension that has accelerated it and made it turn into hysteria. That is a weakness of your own system.

Meditation will definitely improve such a condition, if the excess heat is naturally released. If you are natural, as I told you, then you are safe and there is no god or demon trying to possess you. It is your own nervous system. It is safe to do meditation and you shall receive benefit from it.

Q: Many people meditate and have no side effects, but others have visions of different kinds. Are those visions real?

Master Ni: If your meditation has no effect, it means you have narrowed it down to sitting meditation only. You might try a standing meditation. Sometimes standing meditation brings more benefit than sitting meditation. Sitting meditation is not suitable for all young people. They are so active that sitting still makes their minds become wild, which causes disbenefit. Or it makes them become too thoughtful and they carry their emotion into meditation, which is counter-productive

Once you slow down your body, your mind becomes active, so if you have no way to cope with an active mind, you defeat the purpose of meditation. Do walking meditation or standing meditation or learn *chi kung* forms such as the Eight Treasures or the different styles of *t'ai chi*. You can consider these as meditation, if your mind can concentrate well. *T'ai chi* movement is usually too long for most people, so they do better with a single movement that is slowed down and repeated.

As you mentioned, some people see visions of different kinds in meditation. That is associated with psychology. If you bring your fears into meditation, then they will transform into images. Your own mental projections will associate with your imagination to become visions. Generally there is nothing really there.

Q: Master Ni, in your books, you say that ghosts and spirits can be real, but now you deny that such things are real when they happen in meditation. Why is that?

Master Ni: I do not want you to misunderstand. Spirits are mostly natural; they belong to your personal nature or life being. Each individual contains numerous spirits at different levels. They can appear in your meditation or in dreams as people. An unhealthy mind or active imagination will cause your energy to transform differently. For example, some religious teachers ask you to visualize this or that god, this or that Buddha and so forth. Those energies are merely guided to be better looking, more pleasing figures, but they are untrue. Do not incline yourself to see ghosts or gods, no matter what is disturbing you.

Meditation is a serious science that helps you attain health of mind and internal harmony. On a deeper level, you can obtain the kind of development that cannot be obtained by general activities. For example, the mind will reflect subtle images from the environment. People who lead a quiet life, like researchers, are usually more productive and have more fruitful results. This is fundamental.

If you are too sexy and feel aroused, then you will feel drowsy in your meditation and you will have a sexual experience, which is self-defeating. For good meditation, you must learn to manage yourself. Once you develop yourself, you understand the reality of life and of nature. Then you will not be like a bold but ignorant youngster who goes on a safari and comes too close to lions and other fierce animals. You are not safe if you develop an imagination that indulges in unrealities. Your meditation is only safe if you do not project or mix it up with religion or fantasy.

In ancient times, there were many well-meaning religious people who invented stories about natural spiritual phenomena as ways to make people behave. However, those stories have produced only negative results so far.

The Integral Way uses natural spiritual facts of life to

support positive *yang* energy in lengthening the union between one's body and one's spirits so that when you are forced to withdraw from the body, you may be able to withdraw safely.

II

Q: Would you tell us about sages in the past who came to help people regain their balance?

Master Ni: Your question suggests that there were sages whose spiritual guidance and advice was accepted by all people. No sage can accomplish such a mission for all time and all people. I consider spiritual work a universal mission; people are sent on this mission for their own spiritual benefit. It is important to become spiritually awakened and aspire to accept such a universal mission.

The ancient type of individual spiritual mission is no longer effective. Today, everyone who hears me or reads my writing is involved with the improvement and progress of society. We are all involved. We must work together to remove the negative aspects of worldly culture by concentrating on moving in the direction of a heathy life by creating a heathy culture. With this as our spiritual direction, we might accomplish our universal spiritual mission.

In other words, in ancient times, a spiritual leader could say, "I am the messenger of God." Today, no one person is powerful enough to really benefit all people. People must become their own prophets and their own messengers in their own lives and societies. That is the difference between the ancient religious approach and the modern spiritual approach. We must accept these differences and work on ourselves and our surroundings.

In ancient times, a spiritual or religious leader could say, "God has sent His disciples to guide others and spread His commandments. Only through the teaching of His messengers can people know the virtue or existence of the true Lord." They could also claim that saints are messengers who truly work on God's behalf. We know that nobody is truthfully achieved enough to act on behalf of the Lord God. The true lord is the spiritual nature of each individual. God is revealed in the spiritual development of all individuals and in the spiritual nature and growth of the community or society. Spiritual truth is simply the spiritual nature of individuals and the entire universe.

Spiritual teaching and spiritual leadership are no longer matters of hero worship. The true spiritual work is the awakening of each individual to the deep reality of life. Not only wise people have a life after death. That is not to say that after the present life, people have an afterlife in which their soul enjoys blessing or suffers punishment by having pleased or displeased God. Life is the result of the daily behavior and thoughts of each individual. According to the principle of spiritual energy response, one's behavior and thoughts invite blessings and punishment. Old religions talk about God's punishment without educating people to attain their own growth for their own benefit and the blessing of their own surroundings.

No one of correct spiritual development will be so presumptuous as to say, "I alone am sent by God." All people are sent by God, and they are sent with the spiritual enthusiasm with which to improve themselves and the spiritual condition of society.

In each generation, there are sages who are leaders. It might seem like there are only a few sages available to spread their influence among the masses. In my understanding, this is not totally true because a sage may not be known to the masses for generations. Few sages are ever recognized by their own or later generations. For example, sages such as Lao Tzu, Sakyamuni, Jesus, Confucius and Chuang Tzu were not accepted, rewarded, or supported in their own lifetime. Confucius' teaching did not become popular until three or four centuries later, during the early stage of the Han Dynasty, when the government wished to establish strong central control and used Confucius' teaching to support that ambition. As for Lao Tzu, very few people in each generation correctly understand his teaching. Other teachers share a similar destiny, yet among the many who were called sages, you might wonder how much wisdom each of them really had.

It is a fact that sageliness and social success are two different things. Mass leaders can hardly be considered sages. Their very popularity is an indication that a less than sagely approach may have been taken.

My focus is the importance of individual achievement. All individuals, no matter what their achievement, can be valued at least by themselves.

A sage is someone who lives and has a spiritual response to a certain time, but his or her service must wait until different natural leaders can promote it to the masses of society. Although an upright leader can achieve a position of power, their motives are usually mixed.

I would not argue with the fact that it is a natural phenomenon that each generation only gives birth to a few sages, but religious or spiritual leaders can hardly be defined as sages. I believe that many truly achieved ones never left a trail behind them. Because they lived above the reach of the masses, they were not recognized in their lifetimes or even afterwards. Only a few sages have had that opportunity.

Q: Master Ni, how do sages develop themselves?

Master Ni: This is a vast subject. The great sages like Lao Tzu and Chuang Tzu said that high sages could not be known unless they taught and wrote. However, teaching and writing are not necessarily the signs of a sage. Usually, the things we learn serve us only for a short while. The deep truth cannot be learned from books alone, but as a direct subtle revelation in your own sagely mind. Even if someone has writes down their inspiration, the enlightenment is already interpreted and may not be accurate.

In teaching, because language must be used, the direct truth of a sage's mystical revelation cannot be totally conveyed. Language is highly inaccurate. Sometimes people use different words like intuition to describe the experience of mystical revelation. Intuition is a spiritual function; it is higher or more direct than general knowledge and the general mental function, but it still is not the highest revelation. The highest revelation is natural wisdom. You know, but you do not know how or why you know. The difference between intuition and natural wisdom is that intuition still has an object of knowledge, i.e., what you want to know. Natural wisdom has no need to establish an object of knowledge. It is not a reflection, it is a revelation of universal spiritual energy.

However, people have been fooled by some so called sages, prophets, social leaders, or leaders of the masses who proclaimed that they had received a secret revelation from Heaven. If anyone were to carefully examine their thoughts, they would see the worldly motivation behind them. Instead of truth, such self-proclaimed messages are only momentary impulses that are mixed with certain psychological effects. This is why it is recommended that all messages from all prophets be examined and monitored by each believer. Calm yourself down to learn and to judge objectively.

The only possible way to receive the highest revelation is directly through the serenity of your own mind. Serenity cannot be monopolized by any religious group or leader; it is the privilege of anyone who lives a quiet life. All who know the value of being quiet and living in serenity shall receive revelation, whether a big one or a small one, naturally in their own mind. With that development, you can evaluate the teaching of people who have been socially recognized and know for yourself what is true and untrue in their teaching. Your own direct experience, direct learning and direct revelations are more important than the tales in holy books.

Holy books are not a replacement for your own thoughts and personal revelations. They are just proof or a variation of what has been directly revealed in your own mind. My kind of service does not take some idea invented by me and impose it on your mind. It offers to teach you to live quietly. You might try meditating in all kinds of different life circumstances. For example, when you have a problem or there is trouble in society, correct understanding is possible if you eliminate your impulsiveness and become serene. This will allow you to release the force that keeps your mind focused on your own emotional reactions. Once the emotional drive is gone, your pure energy is restored. When that energy reaches a condition of good concentration, a high revelation might happen to you.

Everybody has the possibility to receive high guidance through secret revelation. I encourage you to live in quietude and become your own sage. Once you open your mouth, you are responsible, because everything you teach is a personal expression based on your level of being.

My service is different from other types of teaching. There is no manipulation, no attempt to monopolize your broad study, no barrier established between your relationship with nature, between you and society or between you and your potential development.

All those things are the fruit of my secret revelation. I am responsible for what I am teaching here, but you are responsible for studying the whole picture, the whole thing I have given through years. Do not pick up one word, phrase or sentence and glorify it alone; rigidity and stiffness bring no benefit. They are of no help to either your life or your behavior.

III

The following instructions for sitting cultivation or meditation were written around the time of the Three Kingdoms (220-264). I have developed them for greater understanding.

The one who wishes to cultivate Tao first learns to be able to give up all affairs. Once all external connections are totally stopped, and also when there is nothing which is disagreeable to your mind, you can be calm, peaceful, relaxed and quietly settle down in seated meditation. Look at your mind: if you are aware that a thought has started to rise, immediately eliminate it so that you can return to peace again.

Then look at your mind again. Although you do not have the intention to create a self-disturbance, you may still have scattered and unfocused thoughts. You also need to clean up those things.

It does not matter whether you practice this in the daytime or at night, but practice it diligently. Do not allow such a practice to be interrupted. Only eliminate what stirs up the mind, but allow the mind to lighten itself. Focus your mind upon the unoccupied space of the mind itself, but do not dwell on any special idea or practice. No small technique is worthy of your attention or trust. Constantly allow your mind to remain unoccupied.

In the beginning, this practice is difficult because you are so impulsive. It is hard to slow yourself down and relax. The battle of coming and going of thoughts and physical reactions is like an itch; do not scratch it, even if it continues to itch. Do not give up when you encounter difficulty. After you have engaged in deep meditation for a long time (every day for a number of years), you will become more skillful. Do not be interrupted by anything such as the phone ringing or by life events that could interrupt your constructive habits, otherwise your spiritual attainment from such long practice will be totally wasted.

Meditation is the way to form a calm mind. It makes you ready so that at any time, whether you are moving, standing, sitting, lying, doing things, contacting people, or in a noisy place, you are always at peace and your mind is always unified.

Be careful; if you command your mind too urgently, you will become sick. If the energy cannot move smoothly, you could become insane. When the mind is calm and still, loosen up a little bit. Attune the mind to be not too loose and not too tight.

Practicing self-control is necessary. Practice gentle

control, do not force it. Even if you lose your concentration, you can keep the mind still. Then, when you face noise and disturbance, you will not feel it is hateful. When you are involved with things, you will not be bothered. This is true calmness. Also be careful; do not think that because you are not troubled by doing things, you can become more engaged or more involved.

It is also important for you to know that after you have attained the capability to face noise and not be stirred by it, it is still not a good idea to be where there is great noise. Always keep the mind unoccupied so that it can be a true house. Let your thoughts be true responses. Make the mind like still water or a clear mirror so that only when there is thought do forms appear.

There are many good methods to make your mind self-composed. By so doing, wisdom grows. The fast or slow growth of wisdom is not at your mind's command or demand. Never force yourself, but remain calm. If you look for fast wisdom, it will harm your pure energy. Once your spiritual energy is hurt, then you have no wisdom.

You do not need to seek wisdom; it grows by itself. This is what is called true natural wisdom. Once true wisdom has come, do not use it to show off. Maintain yourself as a wise simpleton. Then, use calmness to help the growth of wisdom, and use wisdom to further calmness; these two beauties will lead you to infinity. If, in your meditation, you have too many different thoughts, you may see many ugly images. However, even if you see beautiful beings, although it is healthy energy, you must still keep calm-minded. Allow there to be no pressure, let no thing cover the delicacy of the opening heart. If you can do that, you are developing. Your old problems will gradually decrease and you will not create any new ones. Therefore, there will be no more obstacles when you break out of the cage of the dusty world. If you constantly practice this, you will naturally approach Tao, the Way.

There are seven stages to attaining Tao, the Way:

Stage one: Your mind becomes calm and concentrated, and you are easily aware of energy leaks from your body and mind which are caused by worldly intention, worldly attachment, worldly interruption. Your spiritual awareness is sharpened and becomes more sensitive at this stage.

Stage two: Your old physical troubles are totally gone; your body and mind feel light and happy.

Stage three: The insufficiency of energy is repaired and your internal troubles of old are repaired. You begin to look younger, and in fact are younger.

Stage four: You live a long and happy life.

Stage five: You refine your form to become high energy, so you become a true being.

Stage six: You refine your energy to become spirits; you can become a high spiritual being.

Stage seven: You refine your spirits to unite with and embody the Way, so you become the highest being. Your clarity becomes much sharpened.

At each stage you progress until you achieve Tao. At that point, your cultivation and wisdom are complete.

Some people meditate for many years, but no stage can be proven. On the contrary, the person shortens their life and makes it wither and become fruitless, but they declare they have attained wisdom and achieved Tao. Practically, they have not. If you want to know how to avoid this, just do not hold onto any emotional problem when you meditate.

About the pursuit of wisdom, here is a poem to end this precious instruction:

Wisdom grows from circumstance.
Fire (spirits) stir by some disturbance.
By being attached to externals,
    one loses the origin.
Once you initiate an idea (a mental projection),
    do not allow your knowledge
    to assist it.
When the mind activates its knowledge,
    knowledge stirs the mind.
The true spiritual nature is unoccupied.
All power will be found from the union
    of knowledge and intuition.

IV

The next piece is also an old instruction which I have developed further. In the beginning it was passed down orally and was not written down until much later.

Everyday Instruction for Internal Cultivation

After a meal, gradually get ready to sit silently alone. Do not allow any idea to stir. Forget everything. Keep your spirits and mind pure - without content. Keep the lips close to each other and teeth biting together. Your eyes should not look at anything, your ears should not listen to anything, but with concentration keep yourself internally attuned to your breathing. Gently and subtly breathe, almost like nothing, but do not let your mind wander. The fire of mind will naturally descend and the water of the sexual system will rise. You will feel a sweet dew (sweet saliva) in your mouth when your spiritual energy unites with your body. This is the root of a long life. However, in all twelve energy hours,[3] you become pure, as long as you keep pure and quiet. When there is nothing in the Soul Terrace (your

---

[3] Each energy hour is two hours long; thus it refers to an entire day of 24 hours.

mind, usually the forehead region), this is called being pure. When there is no idea or motive being stirred up, it is called being quiet.

The body is the house of energy. The mind is the dwelling place of the spirits. Once your intention moves, your spirit moves. When your spirit moves, your energy becomes scattered. When your intention stays still, your spirits stay. When your spirits stay, then your five *chi* (five elemental energies from the internal organs) gather to become the Golden Immortal Medicine. You may hear noises inside the body. It does not matter whether you move, sit or lie, you always feel that there is wind inside the body. In your abdomen, the noise sounds like thunder. When the energy inside becomes harmonized, you feel the sweet dew (I am referring to the internal energy movement) coming down from the head to the stomach like taking medicine. You hear wonderful music that comes from no instrument. The energy and spirits have intercourse and make you pregnant with spirits. Then you can see your internal territory. Your spirits communicate with you, and your body becomes a pure and wonderful house. You live with the divine one. You must refine your energy many times to become a great medicine. Your spirit can enter and can stay. You live long; you attain light to equal the sun and the moon. Your soul becomes indestructible.

Each day without fail you must keep pure and quiet. *Chi* is the mother of *sen* (spirits); *sen* is the son of the *chi*. Just like the hen that hatches the egg, you always need to be there to nurture your *chi* without deviation. How wonderful it is when you feel yourself become more and more subtle.

In the human body, there are seven precious treasures that make the kingdom strong. The people enjoy prosperity when their energy is full. Sexual essence is the mercury and blood is the gold. *Chi* is the diamond; marrow is the crystal. The brain contains spiritual particles like precious sand and the kidneys are like precious seashells. Your mind and heart are coral. These seven precious things are gathered and return to you, so you can refine them to become great medicine. All spirits inside of you become immortal.

(The above piece of writing is called "Internal Instruction.")

V

Everyday Instruction for External Cultivation:

There is another piece called "External Instruction," which is for your personal protection when you engage in spiritual cultivation. I have developed it for clarity. It says:

Respect Heaven and Earth. Value the sunlight and the moonlight. Obey national customs, culture and rules. Respect your father and mother. Treat those who are above you with humility. Treat those beneath you with harmony. What is right and good should be done; what is bad and evil should be stopped. Help people who wish to learn. Stop people who are destructive. When you are in a high position, be aware that you might fall if you do wrong. If you acquire material possessions, you must be aware not to allow them to go over the rim. Learn to be quiet and peaceful. Learn to be frugal and self-content. Have no worry. Be tolerant. Give up what is luxurious and nurture what is truthful. Stop talking about other people's wrongdoings and praise their virtue. Give small help when you are able. Make peace with your neighbors and stay close to those who are wise and virtuous. Avoid over-enjoyment and indulgence in all kinds of fun. If you do not do well materially, be conservative and fulfill your duty. If you are rich, help other people. Treat all people equally; do not depend on force. Learn how to conquer yourself, and never become jealous. Do not be greedy or scheming. Try to dissolve any resentment or trouble that you might have with others. Accumulate virtue.

Once you make a promise, keep it. Always have sympathy for the wronged and the helpless. Help those who are poor or in trouble. Quietly, secretly, accumulate spiritual merit. Be kind and generous. Do not kill without reason. Listen to good advice; do not cheat your own heart.

Follow these suggestions. They will help you protect your internal practice, so that you will safely achieve yourself.

VI

The Great Understanding

Great understanding can provide you with spiritual help, but it takes time to prove such subtle truth to yourself.

What was born before Heaven
*   was born with no form.*
After Heaven,
*   it lives with forms but does not rely on forms.*
Although it has no form, it moves.
Therefore, it is unthinkable.
When you are quiet,
*   the quietness is your spiritual nature.*
The mind lives within quietness.
When you move, you know it as the mind.

Spiritual nature is within the mind.
When your mind becomes active,
*   your true nature is hidden.*
When your mind is inactive,
*   your spiritual nature appears.*
Like empty space,
*   signs of your spiritual nature are not apparent.*
It can only be comprehended as clarity and wholeness.

The great way has no shape;
*   the great way is shapeless.*
It is absorbed by being.
True nature is inactive.
Externally it gives birth to the mind.
It is just nature when it is quiet.
It is boundless.

When you face a situation,
forget the situation so that you are not entrapped
by the Six Thieves (the five senses and the mind).
When you live with dust,
be above it,
so you are not entrapped by changing conditions.
When you reach the depth of quietness,
you are unmoving.
When you reach harmony and peace,
you are unchanging.
Your wisdom sheds light in all directions.
You return to be unoccupied,
and spiritually you need to do nothing.

Here is a short verse that complements the above instruction:

From the Way you come to know there is no Way.
From doing nothing
you come to know there is something
that must be done.

The Way contains the forms of all things,
however, it is not attached to a single form.

VII

Q: Master Ni, these special instructions are helpful, but short meditation seems unable to produce the same results that the ancient sages achieved.

Master Ni: Meditation was conventionally used as a religious tool to support either a person's fantasy or extended periods of sitting. However, under those conditions meditation is usually fruitless if you wish to experience the Golden Flower.

Q: You once mentioned that some people have three "flowers," but you never mentioned the Golden Flower and its significance in cultivation. Would you explain that now?

Master Ni: Sometimes meditation becomes a means for entering a trance. There are two types of trance. One type darkens the mind and makes it go blank. This is only a type of mental escape that fossilizes your mind or consciousness. The other type of trance is mediumistic in which a spirit or ghost is channelled. This is not spiritual achievement.

I heard of a certain Zen practitioner who could remain in *samadhi* for as long as seven days, but this is bad for one's physical condition, and he suffered from sickness for a long time. I consider this an unnatural state of being. I do not promote such special achievement, if you think it is either special or an achievement.

My attitude is to enjoy each minute of life no matter what the situation, because all situations are transitional. However, cultivating tranquility of the life substance or *chi* is useful and beneficial.

Meditation can sometimes bring about a special experience. Whether positive or negative, disturbing or enjoyable, you can only consider such experiences as part of the process of developing mental maturity. There is no value in singling out one such experience and promoting it as a new faith or religion.

The masses are always waiting to be fed by someone. A teacher can always find followers by emphasizing his or her special experience, but that is not really beneficial to one's own growth or the growth of others. When you medi-tate, I suggest you keep a personal record of your experiences if you think they are special. This will display your experiences before your well-ordered, calm mind and help you safely evolve without holding onto or becoming stuck in one or more personal experiences.

I do not encourage you to do long meditation. Even if you sit for two or three hours at once, the optimum amount of time to help you achieve balanced concentration still lasts only 20 to 30 minutes. Please pay attention to the term I use here: "balanced concentration." Practice it for a comfortable period of time.

I do not tell you which points or *chakras* to work on in your meditation, but I do suggest that you remain in a good sitting position and remain passive in mind. This will allow the different channels, special spiritual points and *chakras* to open up by themselves and blossom as the Golden Flower, which is newly converged spiritual energy displaying itself as a golden light on the head. This is the flower of one's transformed sexual energy. It is a natural consequence that happens without any artificial attempts.

Any particular emphasis or pursuit in meditation usually becomes difficult and strenuous. Some people use long periods of meditation to engage in mental and spiritual exploration. I agree with sages who practiced the type of meditation I recommend here. They scolded people for using meditation as a means of mental exploration. I myself have benefitted from this warning. Their scolding is sweet. I have positive and negative experiences when I fall asleep when meditating all night long and my mind is not guarded. The sages said that the play of the mind, indulging in creating illusions, is negative rather than positive. This means that we can learn to project our mind in a positive and balanced way instead of allowing it to constantly wander in directions suggested by psychological expectations, intellectual or emotional curiosity or internal physical pressures. Such things will create suggestions in dreams or half-dreams. A wandering mind will make you a dreamer instead of someone who faces the reality of life. That is a negative use of that great organ, the brain.

You might like to know the positive use of meditation. First, it can produce physiological self-alignment. Second, it can train the mind in well-disciplined calmness. Third, it can further the evolution of the mind or brain. Fourth, it can improve your mental health and ability to focus. All of this happens naturally when all external and internal influences and conditions are under control. I strongly recommend Natural Meditation for your health, beauty, peaceful emotion, balanced vision and mental development.

Above all, if you know how to decrease your sexual

activity and sit straight and upright, your sexual energy will transform into nutrition that fertilizes the brain and becomes light energy. The Golden Flower is attained from the White or Silver Flower. Strong sexual energy, once electrified, appears as white light. Wisdom, or pure light, is the flower of the mind.

Internal transformation, in Hindi, is called *kundalini* and there is a type of practice that can force that energy to rise to the brain. In Chinese folk Taoism, there is a similar practice. However, I feel that such practices are not as true or safe as allowing the energy to rise gently by itself. If you try to force the *kundalini* to rise, and the unrefined or partially refined energy that rises is too strong, it could push one to the verge of insanity. Such energy has right fruit and wrong fruit. The right fruit is genius or talent; one might become a poet, develop healing powers, musical talent, or a talent in science. The wrong fruit is insanity or perversity.

Energy phenomena should not be your goal. Meditation needs the right goal, the right purpose and the right practice. I advise you to allow energy transformation to happen naturally and benignly without risking unnecessary problems.

Long ago, Pao Po Tzu (Kou Hong) said to refine your sexual energy to assist your brain. It is interesting that some scholars deny this possibility. Surely one's sexual fluid can never flow upward through the spine to the brain, but this energy can be vaporized and electrified. Thus, it is transportable.

A friend of mine played professional basketball in Taiwan and was therefore physically active under sunshine. However, the sexual fulfillment of oriental basketball players is not the same as that of American players.[4] My friend told me the difficulty he had because of seeing golden light in

---

[4]Master Ni is referring to an American basketball star, who publicly estimated that he had sex with 10,000 women during his career.

front of his eyebrows. Most of the men on his team had the same problem, Because they did not know how to manage themselves, they masturbated to relieve this physical difficulty.

Q: Is your point that when it is electrified, it must be under the correct conditions? Also, is natural meditation the better way to electrify this energy?

Master Ni: When this energy is not electrified, it becomes fiery in individuals who cannot maintain a restful state. This is totally different from the sublimation that can be achieved in Natural Meditation. The purpose of Natural Meditation is to balance watery energy and fiery energy so that they supplement each other and produce perfect health. This cannot be achieved by modern sports, which tend to make the body "fiery." The practice of Natural Meditation is symbolized by the ancient *T'ai Chi* Symbol:

Once strong sexual energy is electrified, it can penetrate the brain as random thoughts and cause a disordered flow of electrical current. If this damages the normal current in the brain, insanity is experienced. Visions, light or beautiful scenes in strong light, whether useful or negative, are all the result of sexual energy rising to the brain.

The ancient achieved ones wrote detailed guidance for sexual energy transformation. There are two important guidelines. One is to keep your sexual energy healthy. That is the source of one's talent or wisdom. The second is the correct practice of such a transformation. In a word, be natural. Natural Meditation, as I have described it, meets all safety requirements. Anyone who follows it will not risk insanity. If you do not feel comfortable during your meditation, keep your mind calm and do not think any strange thoughts, that could create an irregular energy charge in the mind. Simply take a walk or do another type of meditation instead of straining to concentrate.

The Chinese term for *kundalini* is "Reversing the Flow of the Yellow River" or "Pumping From the Well." If you sit quietly with your spine straight and upright, allowing the process to occur naturally, it will happen safely and you will still be in command of your calm and quiet mind.

If you have a weak organ in your body, you might apply gentle attention to that spot or region to help strengthen it, but there is no need to be too concerned about it, because that could cause congestion. If you do not have any specific weakness, just sit with gentle wakefulness. This alert sitting is called "*tsun sen*" in Chinese. In English, it means to keep your spirits centered.

In your meditation, it is totally unbeneficial to fall asleep and have an unexpected dream or contorted vision. Although you might have a good story to tell, that is not the correct fruit of meditation. I do not suggest that you use *mantras* in your meditation. When you sit in meditation, the only important thing is to sit with peaceful, harmonious pleasure and have a balanced mood. It is not a good idea to dwell on thoughts that might irritate you before you sit. If you do that, then you become formed, and that kind of emotion is unbeneficial. It could take days to untie the tight muscles of your newly shaped long face.

If you happen to have a trance, recognize it as a phenomenon. Do not accept the old religious attitude that a trance is something special, because that has not been verified by anyone who is wise.

Q: Sometimes when I sit (not always with a straight spine) I experience flashes of light, either inside or outside of my room, or sometimes in my eyes. Is this positive or correct?

Master Ni: It is a positive result. Chuang Tzu reported that when your vision changes, even an empty room seems brightly lit. I would say that it is a special, subtle light that does not come from an external source. That is good progress you have made. Do not expect it, but allow it to grow by itself.

Some people say that meditation cures certain physical problems, but I suggest that you take care of any health problems by seeking good medical treatment. Automatic self-repair work can be done, if it is small or just starting. It is true that the power of self-healing is higher in people whose life is less disturbed than in people who live in the modern world of traffic and high tech communication. I still think meditation can be a helping approach when you have a good healer to take care of you. After you get well, you can use your renewed health to help your meditation, and use the meditation to help improve your health.

In meditation, do not expect ecstasy, and do not use any drug, stimulant or electric device to cause the response of a certain group of nerves. Nothing should interfere with the natural course of your meditation. There is only you, no drugs, no machine, only you. Your complete well-being and your good development can be helped by doing Natural Meditation.

VIII

Q: Master Ni, is the practice of natural meditation a traditional practice or is it your personal preference? My impression is that "Golden Immortal Medicine" is the essential teaching of your tradition.

Master Ni: The practice of dynamic Natural Meditation came to me from generations of accumulated experience and development. It is the teaching of Golden Immortal Medicine without the emphasis on the union of *yin* and *yang*. *The Story of Two Kingdoms* can help you understand the union of *yin* and *yang*. Natural Meditation is what unifies the two kingdoms.

Ancient culture is rich in spiritually developed terminology. When it comes to us, we need to know the difference between the truth and a gimmick. I have tried to clear up the confusion by reviewing, testing, and filtering this heritage. I choose the best and discard what is useless or unimportant. If anybody achieves themselves, it is not by any small technique that attracts their emotions, but by something that touches on the real essence. Natural Meditation is the broad, safe way to success.

During the Tang Dynasty there was a recluse, Ssi Ma Chen Ching who, when he was alive, was recognized by the emperor as a Heavenly teacher. He produced an essential instruction called "*Tien Yin Tzu*." I offer you his instruction, which I have developed for your better understanding in practicing meditation. The teaching contained in *Tien Yin Tzu* can protect you, and can also be used to verify your attainment. It can be beneficial and useful if you read and receive it carefully.

Tien Yin Tzu
One: How to Become a Spiritual Immortal

All people are born with spiritual energy, but through different pursuits and different contact with the world, many of them apply that energy in different directions. They may become knowledgeable about many things or become powerful in society, but they lack a connection with their own deep spiritual self. What is called spiritual means that the light of one's own spiritual vision is not stagnant or separate from the subtle reality of one's own spiritual being. This light enables you to know your own and other people's lives. You can also gather spiritual energy so that it stays with you. Once you are spiritually centered, you can shine this light on all things in your life. If you do this, you have grown above the level of general life. Spiritual cultivation can enable you to become a deep, high sage and can enable you to know and continue your life even after your physical form ceases to exist.

A spiritual being or spiritual person is also a human

being. Because of the focus upon spiritual cultivation, he or she is not contaminated by worldly experiences and can still maintain the naturalness of life. He or she will not become stagnant due to any bias.

Two: Easy and Simple

The way of Heaven and Earth, the Way of the universe, is easy and simple. The sky is above us; the earth is beneath us. When the path opens up, everything appears to us. The simple truth of the universe does not attract us by adornments. It is easy and simple. Thus, it is easy and simple for an achieved one to see the truth.

You may want to know in what way you can achieve it, but you may not even know what the achievement is and whether there is any way that can help you. You do not achieve a discipline, but a new reality.

Whoever learns to be a spiritual being first learns the most simple and easy truth. If someone talks to you with lofty words about strange fantasies, that will only make you stubborn and perplexed and you will not return to the original truth. In that case, you are not learning the easy, simple truth; you are learning something psychological, which is different.

Three: The Gateway Is Gradual

Gradualness is the gateway. Hexagram #53 in the *I Ching* is called Gradualness (Wind or Wood above Mountain) which symbolizes the principle of learning the Way. People who wish to learn the truth and reach the core of their own selves cannot suddenly become wise. Learning the truth must be done step by step. Achievement does not depend on sudden jumps or leaps; you must take it easy. Just keep practicing. By observing yourself, you will gradually enter the depth, and see the truth.

There are five steps in the gateway to Tao. The first step is to fast. The second step is to settle yourself down. The third step is to keep your attention focused. The fourth step is to dissolve the self. The fifth step is to untie your spiritual bondage.

What is a fast? Fasting means to cleanse yourself by making your body clean and making the mind peaceful and empty by avoiding things that confuse you.

What is settling yourself down? Settling down means to stay in a quiet, clean place.

What is keeping the attention focused? Keeping the attention focused means gathering your mind back to your life being.

What is self-dissolution? Self-dissolution means to forget the form and forget the self.

What is spiritual untying? Spiritual untying means you can easily reach the subtle sphere or subtle reality.

You must learn these five steps. First you achieve step one, then step two. After you have achieved the second step, you achieve the third, fourth and fifth steps. This is how you will succeed in spiritual cultivation. However, you must keep doing it; you cannot come back to live differently. That would be going in a different direction.

Four: The Fast

Fasting does not mean only eating vegetables. A complete fast means to prepare yourself by cleansing your body and massaging it so that the blood circulation reaches the skin. Do not overeat or eat strong spices. People receive their life energy from the energy of the five elements; what you eat is the ingredients of the five elements.

You start by becoming a fetus in the womb; then you are born as an independently formed life. You breathe and have internal blood circulation.

In fasting, it is not recommended that you totally stop eating. That is not the way to longevity.

There are spiritual practices to stop eating food and merely intake energy. That is a temporary measure, and does not mean that you never eat anything again. There are spiritual requirements for eating: the food must be clean, good, fresh and free of fats and oils, salt, spices and sugars.

And the quantity must be right. Eat when you are hungry, but do not overeat. Do not eat unripe food. Do not eat or use too much seasoning. Throw away any food which is decayed and do not eat food that makes you feel stagnant.

While fasting, rub your skin often and let the stagnant "cold" moisture go away. Also, avoid sitting too long, standing too long, laboring too long or doing any one thing for a long time; this is so that you can channel your energy and maintain a healthy body. If your body is not troubled, your energy itself will be complete.

Five: Settle Yourself Down

What does it mean to settle yourself down? It does not mean owning a beautiful house with expensive furniture and many luxuries, etc. It means to settle down in an appropriate lifestyle. When you meditate, sit facing south, and sleep with your head to the east. The light in your house should not be too light or too dark. The beam of the house should not be too high, because then the *yang* energy will be too strong and too light. The beam of the house should also not be too low, because then the house will be dark and the *yin* energy will be too strong. If the house is too light, it will hurt your *Po*, and if it is too dark, it will hurt your *Hun*. In people's internal energy, the *Hun* is *yang* and the *Po* is *yin*. Positive, healthy *yang* energy needs to be protected. If it is damaged by too much light or a lack of light in the house, you shall have no peace.

Climate changes can sometimes cause too much *yang* or too much *yin* to be in the house. You need to protect the house from such changes.

The ones who cultivate their life have this basic knowledge.

Where you live should have windows on all four sides. When wind comes, close the windows on that side. When the wind stops, open them. Where you sit, there must be some protection from the wind or light such as a standing divider in the back or bamboo screen in front. If there is too much light, adjust the screen to make you feel peaceful internally. If it is too dark, adjust the screen to make the outside light come in. Or, you may have curtains which you open and close to let the light in or keep it out. Internally, make your mind comfortable, and externally make your eye peaceful. Once your eye and heart (mind) are peaceful, your body will also be peaceful. That is all connected with the condition of light and darkness.

Do not think too much or have too many desires. Otherwise, how can you pacify your internal mood and keep yourself in a good external posture? To learn the Way, you must make yourself sit down correctly.

Six: Keep Attention in Your Mind

What you keep in your mind is the pure spirit. There should be no thoughts, because when the spiritual energy functions, it naturally sees. When you close your eyes, you will feel the existence of your eyes; when you collect your mind, you will feel its existence. Your mind, your eye, should not leave the form; by this I mean, your thoughts and vision should not leave your body. Allow nothing to harm your concentrated attention. If your eye sees people, especially if people attract you or if you keep having thoughts about people, this means that your mind is wandering outside. All day long, people's minds run around in the world because the eye always looks outside. When people habitually use their light outwardly without ever collecting it within their own being, they are weakened and will die young. Returning to the root is accomplished by staying quiet. Quietude is the key to life.

When you enrich the spiritual energy that always lives within you, the gate of all wonders can be found. This is done by simply keeping the mind aligned with the life form.

Seven: Sitting and Self-Forgetting

Self-forgetting does not mean that your energy is scattered. Sitting and self-forgetting start by gathering your spirit back to yourself. When people are one with the Way, they do

not see it. When you are one with Tao, you do not see or
know the Way any more. When you are one with yourself,
you can also be no self. It means you are in spiritual cultivation or meditation; you are awake and aware, but you
do not know you are aware. That is called forgetting. It is
called "non-action," because your mind is not motivated or
active. What is called "seeing nothing" in meditation means
that your spirits and your form have merged, so you see
nothing.

The question is, how can we keep the mind from becoming motivated or active? The internal movement of
people's thoughts is a pattern of dialogue. Internally, there
is always a discussion going on. You keep talking to and
answering yourself. Most people never stop talking to themselves in their minds. We can keep the mind from becoming
motivated or active by ceasing the internal dialogue.

How can you make your mind, body and spirit disappear? By not looking at them. This means, when you do
not establish any internal existence, then you see nothing.

If Tao truly is yourself, do you still need to wonder who
you are? If you wonder who you are, you and Tao are two
things. Once you ignore one thing, and you do not try to
decide who you are, and you also do not try to decide
where or what Tao is, then you do not need to search for
it again and again somewhere else.

Eight: Spiritual Untying

A fast can cause spiritual tension before attaining spiritual
untying. Spiritual untying is attained by strong discipline;
supported by spiritual faith in yourself, you can untie
yourself from the external world. Settling down peacefully
is attained by finding your own freedom from any disturbance or discomfort. Keeping your attention on your form,
you untie yourself from worry. Sitting and forgetting is a
way to untie yourself from frantic thoughts and activities.

When you have faith in your life, calmness in your form,
peace, freedom, and wisdom. You have reached the spiritual throne directly.

What does *sen* or spirit mean? The spirit inside of you is interesting. You do not need to move, but it can reach everywhere. It is not in a hurry, but it is so fast. The spiritual and the physical spheres and the third sphere of the combination of *yin* and *yang* are lasting. A simple human being can reach all three spheres of the universe; it is easy to do that in the deep sphere, once you develop spiritually.

Treating all external things as equal is called morality. Then your personal self-nature becomes one with the nature of universal being. The suchness of truth is exactly the same as your well-being at all levels of life. By returning to non-doing, your self-nature is reached. The functions of nature do not rely on you. It is your responsibility to eliminate whatever motivates you unnaturally. That is applying your nature.

Achievement is born from ease and simplicity. One dissolves one's form with ease and lives to respond equally to all things. This is important, because we typically respond only to the things we like. When you keep in mind that everything is equal, then you are not special, you are not bothered, and you are not partial to anything. When you are active, you are the life of the world. When you are quiet, you are still the world.

Falseness is any deviation from nature. Truth is maintaining the true self. Life, death, movement, stillness, falseness and truth can all be dissolved by spiritual achievement. It is called untying your spirits. Once you are achieved, when you are on the human level, you are a human immortal. When you are in the sky, you are a heavenly immortal. When you are on earth, you are an earthly immortal. When you are in the water, you are a water immortal. You are so transformable, because you are a spiritual immortal. People can become spiritually immortal through the five steps, but they really only need to go through the doorway of gradualness.

Good meditation done in the right amount is positive. If you meditate for too long, it starts to become negative. You do not like to talk or to work any more. Your whole body becomes dissolved like mud in water; you cannot gather your strength because you do not like to engage in any physical activity. You become too lazy to engage in productive activity, so you become like a rubber man or woman. The point of meditation is quality, not time. For modern people, twenty to thirty minutes is a good length of time to concentrate. I would like you to keep this in mind. When meditation is combined with *Dao-In* movement, the result will be even greater. You will achieve the balance of mind and body; a healthy spirit is based on that. This is the fundamental direction to pursue.

All benign stimulation and useful creations are helpful for the brain. Taking a walk and listening to good music are also agreeable. I promote meditation as a supportive practice, not as a lifestyle. The source of a long and happy life is an appropriate amount of useful physical and mental work. Let meditation assist your life; do not use it to spin a cocoon around your life.

Q: Master Ni, meditation is usually promoted as a religious practice. Thank you for making it so simple and clear for us.

Master Ni: In the past, meditators created religion as a tool to educate the masses. Meditation is a tool to be used in general life. You can do it as a type of exercise in your daily life without making it part of any religion.

The main principle of Natural Meditation is to apply the whole *Tao Teh Ching* in your life. The main principle of the *Tao Teh Ching* is to embrace the simple essence of life. This is the most important element of life.

Too many external pursuits create confrontation, conflict and contention in the world. The simple life essence that Lao Tzu called *Poh* is inside of you, not outside of you. Keeping this truthful knowledge in mind, all external pursuits become secondary.

Religions teach meditation as a way to worship God, yet the true God is the simple essence of your own life.

The entire universe developed from the simple essence. Religions teach meditation to liberate your troubled mind, yet you must understand that you were not born with that trouble; it was caused by your own needs and the influences of the external world. Sometimes you create trouble by overextending yourself externally. However, instead of wasting your energy by striving for more power, money, fame, physical pleasure or stimulation, you might learn from the teaching of the Integral Way. One who embraces the life essence regards all other things as secondary.

I teach the principles of the *I Ching*, which expresses balance in life. Each person needs some time for quietude alongside all of life's other activities.

Tao is the universal law of self-balance. The intention of a true teacher is not to make you into a personal follower or believer, because that is of no use in your life. Instead, a true teacher helps you learn to value your personal life essence through a balanced life, and to treat external and internal things correctly.

It does not matter how long you meditate, effectiveness comes from constancy. Every day, whenever you have time available, collect yourself and put yourself inside of you before you make your next move. That will help you clearly observe your own actions, movement and behavior so that you do not need a god, a government, or a policeman to watch you; you become the authority of your own life. When you can manage yourself without causing trouble for yourself or other people, you are god.

The correct conception of God is your own healthy being and the healthy being of the world. "God" is the supportive nature of all lives. When you cannot align yourself to the eternal truth of the Way, then you are far from health.

Many teachers, through need or intention, over-emphasize small techniques to create a group of followers around themselves. When people tell you they have achieved or learned certain esoteric techniques or other gimmicks, and tell you how powerful they are, you should think twice before accepting them at face value. Words can confuse people, thus it is important to learn from those who have real achievement. People who are really achieved do not use words to show off.

The only worthy practice is to embrace your own life essence. If you do so, you shall become wise and have the power to rise above any technique or ritual. If you wish to become spiritually powerful, you must directly embrace your spiritual essence.

IX

When I published the *Workbook for Spiritual Development of All People* years ago, I gave postures and other means of body alignment for meditation. That book was well accepted, even though I did not specifically talk about meditation. In *Gate to Infinity: Realizing Your Ultimate Potential*, I offered Natural Meditation to conclude my introductory work, and I have given even more details about it in this book, *Spring Thunder*.

One of the achievements which comes from doing Natural Meditation is the ability to see scenes of the future or some event in another place. Your eyes are projectors of your mind which wants to know, and at the same time, you are the onlooker of the image projected by your eyes onto a blank section of wall. You focus on a spot to see the scene of an event, then you know the information. After you become more developed, you can find your information from looking at your own palm. Still higher and more direct, you do not even need to use either a wall or your palm as a spiritual "television screen;" your own forehead is the screen. The projector, the onlooker, the gatherer and the giver are all one. The onlooker and the gatherer are newly developed spiritual functions. The projector and the giver are also newly developed spiritual functions, but they are not the same. They are new spiritual developments. This is precious to attain, and an interesting phenomenon in a life, but please do not abuse it once you develop it.

You can still achieve beyond this. The projector, the

giver and the gatherer of the information converge to give voice to an intercommunication between the mind and the upper God who lives in you as part of your body. The Inner God moves to your forehead to offer you the spiritual consultation you need for all types of trouble. No science and no religion can achieve this. This is the flower and fruit of your own spiritual enterprise of self-cultivation.

Natural Meditation does not encourage you to go into a trance or set up the conditions for trance. Natural Meditation is the cultivation of wakefulness. Wakefulness in meditation is similar to the flaming tongue of a lamp. You tend the flame well, and you unite with the gentle flame. Then the light grows to draw support from different levels of energy (such as the oil lamp or the candle) of your life being. Step by step, Natural Meditation has the potential to enable you to see the light change in your surrounding. You may see a gentle white light. You may also see your inner sun and inner moon, and then later you may see the shining silver-gray light. Going further, you may see the golden light that is sometimes called the Golden Flower, which envelops the entire self inside and outside with no limitation.

There are some side effects to Natural Meditation. In the process, your memory improves so that you can remember every detail from a long time ago. You can improve your concentration and thus have much greater accomplishment. You can develop clairvoyance and telepathy, which are normal capabilities, nothing special. You may also suddenly become a good writer, particularly in a poetic style of writing. You might also develop healing power, be able to project your soul, bi-locate, or multi-locate. You can also have immediate understanding of any object on which you concentrate. If you remain passive, spiritual beings can communicate with you as an encouragement, without wishing to possess you in any way. You will look young or youthful, you will feel stronger and happier and live longer. You will achieve all the things I have described by working directly on your spiritual well-being.

There is one negative side effect to doing Natural Meditation. Because your memory becomes stronger, your wrongdoings, significant or insignificant, will be recalled unless you purify them by intensified repentance and notice to the spiritual world to request a new opportunity by not doing or being bad or harmful to other people or yourself again. Those memories are also a warning for you to uphold your responsible behavior and good standards. When judgment is internal, punishment will be internal and external too.

Another difficulty is that you become too fast in what you see and know, and your associates or companions cannot keep up with you. That can cause personal difficulty, because you may become too sharp in your reactions, which is hard for other people to tolerate. The sages suggested that after you attain all the advantages, you muffle your light and remain simple and ordinary in order to live harmoniously with ordinary people. Harmonious relationships are always assets. Otherwise, your achievement drives you to live alone and be secluded. I want you to foresee the trouble of all the spiritual achievements you admire.

Influential people, social leaders and rich people are all ordinary people - why not be one yourself? I teach techniques mainly for your health, beauty and peace. Surely, you can get more than that out of it. Anything extra may be considered a side effect which you do not expect.

I have heard many new researchers marvel at the wonders of the human brain. Sometimes they use the term "higher consciousness" to describe the paranormal consciousness of the brain, but unfortunately they ignore the marvelous wonders of the entire life being. So-called paranormal consciousness is actually the convergence of newly transformed life energy of the individual. In modern terms, it is the "evolved" life energy that has been converged to change a person's low mentality to a high mentality. You can be aware of when your low mental functioning becomes high mental functioning. This high mental energy also accomplishes a lot of internal work for the body, like repairing and rejuvenating the internal systems and organs. You do not notice rejuvenation, however, unless you notice that your appetite has increased and your sex drive has not decreased with advancing age. I do not mean to encourage you to eat more and seek sexual expansion, because the foundation of your achievement still relies on good eating habits and restraint from sexual indulgence. If you eat correctly, you do not need to fast, or you may fast only at the evening meal. It is helpful to take periodic retreats and to periodically abstain from sexual activity as long as it does not damage the normalcy of your life function.

More important than diet, however, is to maintain the health and strength of your reproductive capability. There is a skill or practice for keeping your sexual energy alive. There is a correct practice for this, but do not forget your moral condition or your personality. When you gather your life energy together, you must avoid internal conflict or disharmony.

The growth of spiritual knowledge is a key point in your spiritual achievement and safety. It is not difficult for a careful reader or learner to do this by carefully studying my written work.

I do not suggest that you use religious rituals, *mantras* or other similar practices to induce meditation. For people who do not have much time for study and research, the basic principles can be found in Lao Tzu's book. I have written two elucidations of the *Tao Teh Ching:* the *Complete Works of Lao Tzu* and *The Esoteric Tao Teh Ching.*

There are safe, natural, healthy and simple practices in the *Tao Teh Ching.* With guidance, wisdom, understanding and realization, you can either add Natural Meditation or not, because Natural Meditation can be a state of mind that you carry with you.

I want to emphasize that meditation is not the only way to achieve oneself. There are people who are wise, virtuous and natural, and who live an earnest, responsible life; they are natural sages who do not need to wear Buddha, or the

Messenger, or the Son of God, or any saint or prophet on their sleeves. They owe nothing to society; that is how they help society. The happy and comfortable way to achieve oneself is to observe the teachings of the *Tao Teh Ching*, by living a natural, balanced, non-competitive life. Meditation, or any other practice, is just an auxiliary measure to enhance the effectiveness of one's spiritual cultivation. I mention this because I want you to know that the Way is broad. There are alternatives in practice. You will succeed one way or another. Do not feel disappointed when you cannot achieve in a certain way. All the spiritual knowledge I give in my teaching is meant to assure your spiritual success by helping you realize what you have learned through the self-study program in the *Golden Message*.

To achieve yourself, simply maintain a calm state of mind during your decent life activities. If you do so, there will be no need for painstakingly long hours of meditation. The Golden Flower[5] can easily suffer miscarriage if you lose the peacefulness of your life by emotional disturbance.

However, with the practice of meditation in a state of wakefulness, from the progress you made in the different stages, you can see the light converge as your light being. Sometimes, or at the beginning, you see it appear in the exact size of your physical body, but it is much more beautiful, standing or sitting in the subtle light. Sometime later you might see a miniature of your own young joyful life seated on your head; that will bring you ecstasy. It is a natural phenomenon. Once you accept it as normal, then you can manage yourself better. To have a life of light is to enjoy greater freedom. There is no reason to behave crazily.

In the stage before the dissolution of the two partners (the conscious mind and the light body) you can see yourself somewhere. That accomplishment is the convergence of the two. Then, the subtle life of complete independence

---

[5]The Golden Flower is also called the immortal fetus or red baby.

will come naturally. All achievement can be made by align-
ing your lifestyle and reality with the teachings of the *Tao
Teh Ching.* This type of achievement is not like magic, which people
show in exchange for money. This is a step-by-step process
which can be proven by serious spiritual students. My
spiritual advice is to take responsibility for your own spiritual
development and rely on no one. It is just like eating; you
must eat your own food in order to sustain your survival.
No one can eat it for you. Although you can have many
spiritual friends at all levels, spiritually each person must
be self-responsible.

X

If you sit down to meditate when you are pressed for time,
your subconscious and your entire system will react by
feeling rushed or preoccupied. Anytime you are under
pressure, it is not an appropriate time to meditate. When
you are waiting for people and you are not under stress
and can relax, that is a better time to take a break. You
could take a short gentle rest, but not deep meditation. As
long as there is any thought of excitement, your mind will
not be peaceful. Peace is an achievement, not a natural
condition.

Do not turn your meditation into a routine that becomes
a burden. Do not do it unless you have time to do it. If you
make meditation an obligation, like a military drill, it
becomes as unnatural and as negative as religion.

When you sit, do not use a watch or clock, because that
will put you under the constraints of a time frame.
Meditation can help you break out of time frames. In
modern times, people rush around everyday at the bidding
of the clock. They are locked into their schedules. However
useful a schedule might be in daily life, it is incorrect to
put yourself under similar restraints in your meditation.

There are two ways to choose times for meditation.
One way is inspirational: you simply know when to do it,
how long to do it, and when to finish. That usually occurs

when you are highly achieved or you have a better life schedule (I mean you are the boss of your own life). In general, the other way is to use the hours that you are not earning a living working for other people. Those hours are your own time. Even a brief meditation is still the most meaningful thing you can do for yourself.

I have read recent reports from China, where some people who live to be over 100 years have maintained a lifelong habit of doing half an hour of meditation twice a day, once in the morning and once in the evening.

It is not required that anyone do long hours of meditation. However, Natural Meditation does require that you do effective meditation. For people who live in the world and have many obligations to fulfill, I suggest that you meditate several times a day, each time for as long as you feel comfortable. If you have a better life arrangement and are supported to do so, you can meditate more often and for longer periods of time. If you are in a retreat for the purpose of meditation, you can organize your meditation with other useful and meaningful activities such as reading the classics I have elucidated for modern students, sitting, walking, talking and laughing.

Chapter 5

Self-Upliftment to Freedom

Q: Master Ni, I have always loved nature and have ridden horses for many years; they are my friends, and the feelings I have around them are much deeper than I can explain. I can think of four that definitely became attuned to me on a subtle level.

I do not rely emotionally on any animal that comes into my life; we merge, grow and eventually part. They actually have taught me the importance of forgiveness, non-ego, naturalness, and patience.

I want to learn how to merge my spirits the way I merge spiritually with my horse. I actually laugh out loud, it feels so good. The horse becomes an extension of my body and I become an extension of the horse's mind. Nothing in my life can compare to this type of intercourse.

I would like to achieve this spiritually. Any guidance from you would be greatly appreciated. To me, it is something I must do alone, but I would like guidance.

Master Ni: In your personal choice of spiritual practice, please take care.

If riding horses helps your physical condition, there is no reason to stop doing it. Yet, if your focus is only on a physical horse, this seems more psychological than spiritual. Be careful that you do not create a psychological trap for yourself which would then create suffering or downfall. Animals do respond, but if they become sick or die, they will make you suffer. It is better to choose something abstract, not a real thing.

A white cloud in the sky is like a horse. Any white cloud will do. If you imagine the sky as a horse, you shall receive a much more powerful achievement. It is not necessary to imagine that the sky is a horse; you can imagine any healthy image. It is also right to connect spiritually with the universe without any image. Traditionally, there are many images that can help your spiritual health. Select one of the following and use it as a lifetime practice:

1. the red sun

2. a boundless ocean

3. a broad meadow

4. a beautiful tree

5. a beautiful pond

6. a living fountain with crystal clear water

7. a beautiful pavilion

8. a nine or twelve story pagoda or tower

9. a seated jade statue

10. a great human being sitting on a beautiful and comfortable cushion safely and steadily

11. the Three Pure Beings

12. yourself dressed lightly and sitting in the center of an immense, clear land

13. a tiny human figure of pure being on the vast horizon

14. a giant human figure of a pure being on the vast horizon

15. a gathering of all pure beings

16. yourself standing in a wonderful world with all the treasures you can imagine

17. yourself flying freely in the sky

18. yourself sitting in an easy chair in the sky and all its twinkling stars, and you possess the most gentle light

The traditional requirement is to sit upright and visualize this for 24 hours, but I think if you keep the image in your mind and do not forget it as you go about your life activities, it will still be helpful. People are what they imagine themselves to be, thus this practice has a spiritual function. If you practice it too rigidly, you might become religious. I suggest when you tire of doing it, you enjoy just being what you are, a pure being. These practices can help a scattered or lonely mind.

Experimentally, in a darkroom someone put a negative on the forehead of a person with long years of intensive practice, and was able to develop the image that appeared on the film. The highly achieved spiritual eye can see the image in your mind clearly without needing film.

I myself prefer to keep nothing there. I keep purifying my thoughts as they pass through.

The spiritual practice of visualizing a personal spiritual image has a long history. Some African tribes imagine themselves as lions. Native American tribes imagine themselves as eagles. In ancient times, the Han people of China imagined they were dragons. A Chinese dragon mostly represents powerful energy like big storms. A dragon also represents a strong leader like an emperor. At least, the emperor would like to be as strong as a dragon. Generation after generation of Chinese emperors used the dragon as their emblem, similar to western knights who used the lion. Now the eagle has become popular: the American eagle has one head and the Russian eagle has two heads as their power symbol.

I do not consider these to be high spiritual practices. A developed person would adopt no symbol or image to suggest good fortune or misfortune. That is great spiritual progress.

A very timid person might use an image of a monster with a string of skulls around its neck in order to scare other monsters away. It might have a psychological affect on young students, but it is not spiritual achievement.

It is a spiritual achievement to be nothing, so nothing can hurt you. I was taught that if you visualize yourself as one with the environment, then you cannot be seen. There was a spiritual practitioner who visualized himself as water. For years he worked to achieve himself and became famous for his spiritual power, so the emperor sent an officer to bring him to the court. Each time the officer went to the achieved one's cave and looked for him, he saw nothing in his seat but water, so he could not fulfill his assignment. However, someone finally told the officer the secret and he threw a pebble at the water. The achieved one was then seen in his physical form because his emotion responded to the disturbance.

It is spiritual progress to recognize the strongest thing in the world which is undefeatable and undestroyable: nothing. Therefore it is safe to be nothing; it is most powerful to be nothing. It is a kind of advanced spiritual appreciation to dare to accept the practice of nothingness. Typically, most people like to be the most powerful being among all beings, or above all others, such as the king of all kings or the lord of all lords, but all the kings and lords, whether strong or weak, will someday disappear, because no one can last. Thus there is nobody who can be considered the most powerful.

It takes a spiritual student some time to appreciate the image and practice of nothingness. Nothing can destroy nothing, nor can anything be compared to nothing. You might think that beingness can compare with nothingness, but you might notice that all beingness is conquered by nothingness. One must learn to be content to be whatever and wherever one is. The happiness of a gigantic bird, if compared to that of a tiny sparrow, is the same. Be happy with what you are, because that is what you are. You are not something or someone else.

All things have limitations, only nothing has no limitation. No one needs to be the strongest. It is all relative anyway. A Chinese proverb says: "Even if you are strong, there is still someone who is stronger than you. Even if you think you have achieved the highest peak, there is still a higher peak. You can be strong, but not for competition, because you can still find a stronger opponent." To learn Tao is to compare nothing to one's own being. Therefore, "nothingness" is natural to the advanced spiritual student.

Q: Master Ni, your book Nurture Your Spirits *left some loose ends for me. I do not feel the need for many spirits yanking at my sleeves; the subtle level is fine with me.*

Master Ni: I wrote the book *Nurture Your Spirits* because most people do not have true spiritual experience and might deny any reality other than the physical. Also, some people with spiritual experience might mistake their own personal spirits for an external god or other thing. Nurturing your spirits is a scientific approach to self-discovery. Spiritually, you can disassemble your different spiritual agents on all levels to communicate with you, but then you still need to put them back in one piece for higher, further pursuit.

The positive contribution of that spiritual practice is to rejuvenate your life and break through your psychological, emotional or physical blockages. Another positive contribution of that practice is to enable you to know the reality that above the physical form there is an unformed spiritual reality.

If a person has known or hidden mental problems, it is not appropriate to do such a practice. A healthy body, mind and spirit is required. Spiritual self-cultivation through that practice is indirect, but it is scientific. It offers proof to people with a modern skeptical mind.

The easy, safe, and direct way to achieve yourself spiritually is the pure practice of Natural Meditation and other practices such as those in my book *Mysticism.*

Q: I want to develop myself in this lifetime. I may not get to the highest level, but I do not want to come back to the same worldly troubles. I would like to be a peaceful spirit who can help others from a different sphere. The physical world is so limited. I am willing to go slowly, year by year, to reach a more subtle level.

Master Ni: You might like to start by going through the self-study program (correspondence course) of the College of Tao.[6] Later, you might like to join the service of offering the correspondence course to others. This is one direction for your spiritual fulfillment.

Your deep interest is in being a pure and moral spiritual being, a free immortal. It is a new spiritual integration. You need to work for it. Please study my new publication, *Immortal Wisdom* [forthcoming], and my other books related to immortality.

---

[6]Editor's Note: For more information on the self-study/correspondence course, see the "Spiritual Study Through the College of Tao" page at the back of this book.

Chapter 6

Immortal Poems

Q: Master Ni, when you were young, did you know you would become a spiritual teacher?

Master Ni: Not at all. I did not want to be a teacher. I did not have any ambition in this direction. In Chinese culture, spiritual teaching is not a career or a profession, it is a kind of service. I was a reckless boy who was greatly affected by the many wars that tore across China. Those wars made me thoughtful, even though I was quite young. Just like other people who face challenges and difficulties, I became reflective, although I was still reckless. In other words, I did not grow to be artful in human relationships that favored me. I did not have time for that, and it has been a shortcoming in my life.

To be a spiritual teacher requires a special quality that I did not have. I was not born wise, but I kept undauntedly learning and improving myself.

I would like to tell you a story about a man with a similar tendency. Although I am less extreme, I do have a similar disposition. His name was Chahng Yun and he was born during the early part of the North Sung Dynasty (960-1127 C.E.; including the South Sung Dynasty, 960-1279 C.E.). When he was young, he studied books and learned swordsmanship. He was considered capable both as a civil officer and a general, and he was quite a proud young man.

At that time, Emperor Tai Chung (976-998 C.E.) had already decided to personally lead the army against the northern invaders. In the third year of Emperor Tai Chung's reign, Chahng Yun took the government examination. The topic of his composition was "Success Can Be Achieved Before You Send Out the Army." Chahng Yun wrote in his paper, "Store your weapons. Make no use of the drum. There is no need of the power of the army. People will obey you like the wind that blows over the grass because you follow the virtue of nature." He thought that he would become the champion among all the scholars in that examination, but the main examiner thought he was no

119

good and crossed his name off the list. They chose another young scholar, Fu Dan, as number one. Chahng Yun was angry about what happened because it hurt his young pride, so he tore up his scholastic papers and decided not to pursue a public position any further.

Chahng Yun had been a friend of Master Chen Tuan, whose story is told in *The Life and Teaching of Two Immortals, Volume II*. Once Chahng Yun decided to give up his future as a scholar, he went to the Panther Forest Valley of Chung Nan Mountain where he wished to learn from Chen Tuan who was living there at the time. Chen Tuan refused him, saying, "In the future you shall be a public servant with a life of hard work. You are not one of us. At a time when the royal court holds a big banquet with great joy and happiness, the kitchen will suddenly catch on fire and the host and the guests will panic. You will be the one who extinguishes the fire. Your good cycle will begin the year after next, so you should not stay here on a secluded mountain."

Chahng Yun insisted and begged to become Chen Tuan's student, but Chen Tuan told him straightforwardly, "You have a fiery and strong disposition. How can you learn the subtle Tao?"

After several days, Chahng Yun reluctantly bid farewell to Chen Tuan. When he departed, Chen Tuan gave him ten writing brushes, some ink and nice paper and encouraged him to serve society and become a public servant.

He also gave him a verse as a farewell gift:

> *Some day you will re-enter Shu (now Szechuan).*
> *You will be busy putting out the fire*
> > *when most people are making merry.*
> *Later, you will govern a beautiful land*
> > *south of the river*
> *Due to having a lump on the side of your head.*

When Chahng Yun heard this, he did not understand what it meant. Chen Tuan just laughed and said, "In the future, you will understand it naturally."

Years later, Chahng Yun tried again to pass the governmental examination. This time he passed and was assigned to be magistrate of Fu Pei county. For his good work, he was promoted to governor of the Chen Tu region of Szechuan province. When there was an outlaw rebellion there, he successfully led the army to crush it, and the emperor gave him an even better position as governor of Hanchow.

In Hanchow, some ambitious leaders of a religious group started a rebellion and Chahng Yun extinguished the fire of that war. His success earned him an even higher position, and he joined the central government in Kai Fung (now the capital of Huh Nang province).

In the meantime, a large tumor had begun to grow on the side of his head, making it impossible to put his hat on properly so he requested an appointment outside the central government.[7] Emperor Chen Chung told him he could use a soft hat and still attend to government affairs, but Chahng Yun excused himself saying, "I do not want my personal problem to disturb the system." Then Emperor Chen Chung sent him to be governor of Shen Jouh, which is now Nanking in Chiansu province.

Thus, in Chahng Yun's life, everything happened as Master Chen Tuan had foreseen. His intuition of Chahng Yun's personal disposition was also accurate. There is an important guideline in spiritual cultivation: "Do not do evil, even if it is small and insignificant, and do not neglect anything good because of its smallness or insignificance." This principle can be applied to your own self-discipline and cultivation. To apply it to other people would be cruel. Chahng Yun's temper often caused him to lose his self-discipline and hurt others.

Chahng Yun was strict with himself. However, he should only have punished people according to what they

---

[7]At that time, rank in government was distinguished by the type of hat the official was allowed to wear.

deserved, not because he had the authority to think that these people might become worse for making a small mistake.

I used this story to show that I did not choose to become a spiritual teacher, but I did choose spiritual cultivation to improve myself because emotionally my attitudes were similar to those of Chahng Yun. I thought that if Master Chen Tuan were to evaluate me, he would probably consider me the same type as Chahng Yun. I was not really like Chahng Yun, but I know I have the shortcoming of being reckless. I react too fast to most situations.

It is easy for all of us to ignore our own mistakes, but hard to ignore those of other people. Instead of being a strong teacher who teaches and executes discipline, I would like you to consider me your spiritual friend who has sympathy for your mistakes and who encourages you to be correct.

As a youth I was like most young people who are anxious to know what they will be. Although Chinese medicine was my family's tradition, I thought I must do something much greater, and that no one in the world could compare to me, so I looked into different systems of fortune telling in order to know myself. Each time I met a developed person I asked, "What will I be?" I wanted an objective foundation before I imagined anything about my personal development.

One of my father's friends who was accomplished in one system of divination prophesied that I would become a general. China did have a lot of wars, and that was one way people could distinguish themselves. Yet the dreams of a teenager can hardly bring peace to a nation or the world. That was my ambition until I read a line of a poem that said, "When a general receives fame, ten thousand skeletons will have been scattered on the battlefield." Keeping that in mind, I changed my direction.

Another of my father's friends owned a mill. He knew how to tell fortunes also, so at the age of 12 or 14 I started learning how to tell the future. After a while, I knew that fortune telling systems can tell your potential future development. What you actually become is still determined by your own vision and efforts. Correctly applied, fortune telling is a way to describe your life, but your character is up to you.

Most people are looking for money, social position, enjoyment and so forth. These are all things that can be foretold. That is to say, in general, people are predictable. If, however, you decide to be a first-rate human being, do not allow your mind to follow the pattern of ordinary action and reaction. Then you are beyond the calculation of any horoscope.

There are two kinds of people who are not controlled by fortune. One kind is extremely evil and can create misfortune for himself and others. Such people prosper by subnormal means. Their life also ends in a subnormal manner. No general pattern can categorize their lives.

The second kind of person who is not controlled by fortune is the most virtuous. These people give up what they enjoy and take blame or an unfavored position according to their virtue and wisdom. No system can tell when such a person will become rich, powerful, fortunate or happy in love. That is not what they live for. They might choose to shun such an opportunity for righteous reasons, so there is no predictable pattern that can describe them. Those who achieve self-mastery are beyond the calculation of any system. When you live a life that earnestly moves in the direction of righteousness, you are a living God. No one can foretell what will influence your life.

The concern about what kind of life to live led me to study the ancient developed ones. I wanted to learn how they understood life and how they applied their life energy in the area where they had the greatest potential for development. This has nothing to do with money, fame, social influence or popular support. It has to do with a reward beyond material goods or social status. The ancient developed ones pursued their spiritual potential.

This can be summed up in a short sentence: "Attaining

a peaceful conscience is the highest profit you can gain in life." With this fundamental key, I observed many people and saw that most of them had developed false characters in order to please others. There were also some true-hearted people of firm character who enjoyed whatever life and position they had. Godly, divine or sagely are irrelevant descriptions unless you live a truthful life and find contentment in your own simple essence. Master Chen Tuan is one of those who attained the truth of life.

Since we cannot be helped by Master Chen Tuan directly, how can we help ourselves? I have some special life knowledge that was passed down from Master Chen Tuan. You need to decide in which of the following five categories your destiny falls:

1. People who make a living
    or who earn their daily bread.
2. People who seek social recognition or fame.
3. People who seek wealth and power.
4. People who seek virtue and wisdom.
5. People who seek the immortal source of divinity.

Each category has an upper, middle and lower level, and you can choose whichever level you wish.

At the physical or worldly level, you have less freedom than you have at the spiritual level. Spiritually you have more freedom to achieve what you would like to be. Thus spiritually, people who earn their daily bread can also be people of virtue and wisdom. People who seek fame or wealth can also develop themselves to become sages. Virtue and wisdom are still knowable, but those who achieve spiritual immortality and divinity cannot be recognized. On the surface, their lives appear no different from those of ordinary people.

Most people who are born into the physical world are trapped by the need for food and clothing. However, that does not decrease one's spiritual potential. Any interference from your society, family or close friends is no reason not to eventually become virtuous and wise. The highest spiritual attainments of immortality and divinity are not determined by anyone, including yourself, but wisdom and virtue can be attained by anyone who applies themselves with self-discipline and self-opportunity to move toward the light during times of darkness.

When I was a teenager, I knew I must provide food and clothing for myself just like other people. By my own spiritual learning, I came to know that most people can do and be more than that. Many people become financially well-off while fulfilling their material needs, unless they use their physical foundation to go in a direction where there is no competition. By that I mean spiritual achievement.

When I was young, I gathered from my society's beliefs that many sages or leaders were born with extraordinary qualities under special conditions, like Jesus or Sakyamuni or Lao Tzu. What I realized later was that your birth does not restrain you from improvement or self-development. That can be achieved through your own endeavors by using every opportunity available. In this way, you give birth to yourself each day, each month and each year.

To me, being born rich or noble is not more respectable than being born in the "mud," if you give birth to beautiful, pure flowers in your life. Do not be dismayed or sit and complain about what your family and society have offered you. You can achieve something greater if you accept your own spiritual responsibility to do so.

My young heart greatly admired Chen Tuan. When he was young, he decided that if he could not be emperor and bring peace to the world, he would do spiritual cultivation and become an immortal. When I was young, I did not value immortality, because I did not understand it. I shared Chen Tuan's ambition to bring peace to the world, but I was a much rougher person. I reacted to the challenges and pressures of the world the way Chahng Yun did. However, through the teachings of the spiritually developed ones, I was slowly guided to the path of gentleness.

Master Chen Tuan's spiritual influence helped me expand my spiritual learning. I consider myself to have one small portion of him, a great big portion of Governor Chahng Yun, and another portion of modern conditions and circumstances. Since I am hardly a good example, I wrote the *Life and Teachings of Two Immortals* for my beloved friends and readers to learn from.

Poems of Master Chen Tuan and His Friends

I would like to share with you some poems from Master Chen Tuan which I did not put in my book about him. I hope you enjoy them and can find inspiration in them.

When Chen Tuan was 5 or 6 years old, he still could not speak, so people thought he was dumb. One day he was playing beside the water, and a woman in blue took him with her to the mountain. Legend says that the woman had green hair like pine needles covering her whole body, thus she was called "Hairy Lady." Actually, she was a female immortal. Hairy Lady gave Chen Tuan some refined water to drink and from then on, he could speak. This is the poem the Hairy Lady gave to Chen Tuan.

My basket is not full of herbal medicine.
I shall go to the top of the steep mountain.
Your way to return "home" will be given.
Do not search in the deep traceless forest.

She also gave him a book: *The Book of Changes*.

When Chen Tuan lived on Hua mountain, he was friends with a person who had learned from Master Lu, Tung Ping who was called "Master Linen Clothes," because he always wore linen, summer and winter. When Master Chen Tuan first left Hua Mountain, he left one short poem for his friend.

There are two ways to go to Hua mountain.
Where we live,

there are only a few grass houses
and a stream full of clouds.
Tell people that you are deaf to worldly news
about the rights and wrongs of people.
This is how to maintain your virtue complete and long.

This is the poem written by Master Linen Clothes in
answer to Master Chen Tuan's poem.

I sit alone in the grass hut
far away from the glamour of the world.
I do not need a garment and a sacred bowl[8]
like the Zen monks.
I know only one thing:
I do not talk about worldly things when I meet people.
This is how I manage to be left alone
and rise above the world's travails.

Here is another poem by Master Chen Tuan:

At night, the North star and the Southern Cross
turn around and around.
During the day, you see the sun rise
and then set on its non-stop journey.
Worldly life makes people rush around like wild horses.
They chase after fame and money like chickens
in a farmyard searching for food.

Nobody notices bamboo and pine trees
because they stay green all winter long,
but short-lived peach blossoms and white plum flowers
attract everyone's attention.
People are infatuated with momentary beauty.
Who can see through the dream-like, dusty life of the world?

---

[8]In the Zen tradition, there is a lineage of achieved ones. The lineage is passed
from one individual to another by the symbolic giving of a certain type of garment and
a bowl.

*That one can stay where the white clouds live
high on the mountain.*

When he arrived at the palace in the capitol, Chen Tuan was old but he was full of life and fresh spirited. The emperor asked how he could achieve that for himself, and Chen Tuan answered:

*It takes years to learn Tao.
Every day I swallow two great medicines:
the sun and the moon.
I brew an immortal beverage internally
to help keep my sideburns dark.
The immortal peach within me helps me look younger.
During the night, I sleep only at my own place,
which is a place for spiritual cultivation.
In the early morning, I approach the altar
to do my spiritual practice.
Your majesty asks how I cultivate myself.
I am helped by the depth of Hua mountain,
which provides me with leisure and freedom.*

When he stayed in the capitol, many people came to see Chen Tuan for advice because he was a good prophet. At that time, a scholar requested his teaching, and this is what the Master told him:

*Once you are aware of having taken advantage of
being supported by a situation,
never go back to it.
Where you enjoy most,
do not stay too long.
If what you do and are
makes you feel you are great,
do not be there or do that again.[9]*

---

[9]Master Sou Kong Gi (Sou Yung) praised this as being a valuable teaching given to us by a highly achieved person. If we learn to know what is advantageous, we may take it but practically it is a loss of oneself.

The emperor heard about Master Chen Tuan's fondness for sleep and he asked him the spiritual meaning of his sleep. This was Master Chen Tuan's answer:

I like sleep.
I do not lie on a blanket or use a comforter.
A piece of stone is my pillow.
My grass raincoat is my mattress.
I do not pay attention to North, South, East or West.
I am not disturbed by thunder in the sky
  or earthquakes on the mountain.
I am not shocked by the ocean water
  jumping thousands of fathoms high.
I am not startled by the noise of the sea.
In that moment, I just sleep soundly.

The poem did not directly answer the Emperor, but it expresses the spiritual calmness that Chen Tuan nurtured.
Here are two other poems.

I

Learning the Way enables you to become pure
  and become quiet.
From being pure and quiet,
  you learn to calm your spirits.
The absence of greed and attachment
  allows your life to flow.
Do not learn to be mean from the world's fools.

II

The moon is my limb.
Water is my mirror.
I take life support from the long-necked gourd.
I do not need anyone to support me when I'm out or in.
The golden turtle on my left
  and the white crane on my right guide my way.

Chen Tuan returned to Hua Mountain, but the emperor again and again wished to see him. Finally, Master Chen Tuan agreed to see the emperor, and this is how he answered him.

The person who lives on the three peaks of Hua Mountain
 has forgotten how long he has lived there.
The haze and the clouds are his livelihood.
The rosy clouds in the sky
 and water in the stream
 have become his family.
He plants herbs at the side of the glass gazebo.
He plants pines by the side of the creek.
Now he agrees to temporarily leave the immortal caves
 and accept the invitation from your majesty.

I recommend that you recite the next poem.

The Way can be pure.
The Way can be quiet.
From being pure and quiet
 I work for my own centeredness.
I am greedy for nothing.
I am attached to nothing.
I allow my life to follow nature.
I do not learn from fools
 who move a different way.

The moon is my light.
The water is my mirror.
My life root is not anywhere else.
Although there is nobody to escort me in my travels,
 I have the golden turtle and the white crane
  always as my companions.

(The golden turtle and white crane are internal energies that can be developed as guardians.)

The first night after Chen Tuan arrived in the capitol, when he was sleeping he heard the bell and was inspired to write two other poems.

I

The doors of a thousand houses
*   are locked or open.*
Above in the sky, the stars are quiet.
It seems the struggles of the world
*   will take time out to rest,*
*   but you can frequently hear the drum*
*   telling time in the streets.*
The galaxy turns and the night becomes late.
The people lie on their pillows,
*   but their minds cannot rest.*
It is a pity that people run after fame and profit;
*   even in their dreams,*
*   they stay connected with the world.*

II

The dripping measure of the water clock
*   slows to almost nothing.*
The moonlight keeps a thoughtful mood.
The occasional cry of night birds
*   sends the chilly cold from the sky.*
This makes travelers think about home,
*   and also makes some travelers hate to leave.*
Light touches the window and shocks the eyes
*   which are open and can see fame and profit.*
The restless mind that lies against the pillow
*   calculates right or wrong.*
All the powers of kings and emperors
*   are like fleeting thoughts.*
Generation after generation
*   has risen and declined until now.*

The emperor wished to make Master Chen Tuan his

advisor at the royal court, but he could not keep Chen Tuan in the capitol. No matter what he offered him, high position or women, the emperor did not have the power to make him stay. Master Chen Tuan bid farewell to the emperor with this verse.

The high place in Hua Mountain is my place.
Anytime I'm out of the house
  I'm in the sky and riding on the wind.
I do not need any lock on my door.
It is always sealed by white clouds.

Master Chen Tuan was respectfully called "Master White Clouds" by the emperor and has been known by that name ever since.

Master Chen Tuan decided not to go among people any more once he felt his duty was fulfilled. He sang:

I have made my mark in the red, dusty world
  for dozens of years.
I miss the green mountains
  which often enter my dreams.
People who compete for glory
  are rarely peaceful and do not rest well.
The red doors of the palace express nobility,
  but do not seem to me as good as ordinary doors.
It makes me worry to hear that heroes need to use swords
  and weapons to help the declining sovereign.
It makes me tired of the music and the sounds
  which only entertain the drunk.
I will take my poems and return
  to my old hut in the wilderness.
The flowers and birds there present the great spring of life.

Conclusion

Spring thunder is sometimes loud and booming, sometimes gentle and subtle, yet it awakens all hibernating creatures. I hope your deep inner life is also awakened by the time you read my conclusion to this book.

Spiritual teaching in some traditions is confined to narrow rituals and rigid disciplines, but the teaching of the Integral Way applies to all facets of life; it is not limited to the surface but goes into the bones and marrow of all aspects. This ageless heritage is what I have to offer spiritual students of all ages and all backgrounds. Everything I teach can be linked together by the important practice of Natural Meditation.

Q: Master Ni, there are so many techniques for spiritual cultivation. Is Natural Meditation the most important form of spiritual self-cultivation you have taught to people?

Master Ni: In ancient times, spiritual self-cultivation was called The Pure White Enterprise (白業 or 淨業). This was recorded by Guan Tzu (d. 645 B.C.E.), the famous prime minister of the small country of Chi during the period of Spring and Autumn (722-403 B.C.E.) of the Chou Dynasty (1122-249 B.C.E.). Guan Tzu's political philosophy and spiritual knowledge was all gathered into his collection which was called *Guan Tzu*. I have absorbed this precious spiritual heritage into my own work, *Stepping Stones for Spiritual Success*. The Pure White Enterprise is an individual's own spiritual enterprise. It is easy to understand in today's commercial culture; you invest your time, energy and money in the direction of your own spiritual development. I call it spiritual self-cultivation. Is self-cultivation not the most serious "investment" in your life? Is self-cultivation not the most valuable enterprise you engage in, whether you are a scientist, a religious leader, business person or scholar? If you are capable of doing more than merely making a living, and you pursue nothing beyond money, fame, influence and physical pleasure, what you pursue is limited. Overdoing anything has negative side effects that are mostly external. By pursuing those things, you do not serve your essential life, which is your spirit. You should consider spiritual self-development at least as important as one of your investments. It is actually the most profitable business, and no government can ever tax it. The profit is all yours. No one is able to take away the internal kingdom you have created through your own effort.

The Pure White Enterprise has helped many individuals become very developed. Later, we recognized them as People of the Way. Jian Tai Gong was one of them.

At that time, the main leadership of all countries was the warrior class. The high ones followed spiritual discipline. The Pure White Enterprise was the education and self-discipline of the White Warriors or knights. The Pure White Enterprise was not Guan Tzu's invention; he continued and preserved its heritage and work from Jian Tai Gong or Tai Gong Won (ca. 1191 B.C.E.), a well-known achieved one. Jian Tai Gong is usually depicted as an old fisherman; he was a talented recluse who lived near the Wei River and was discovered by King Wen who invited him to be his top advisor. Later, he assisted King Wu in establishing the central government of the Chou Dynasty when it replaced the declined Sharng Dynasty (1766 - 1121 B.C.E.).

At that time, religion was a leader's social service and the Pure White Enterprise was for their individual self-development. The spiritual self-discipline of the warriors is the kind of spiritual culture I wish to preserve. I recommend it to modern spiritual students on different occasions and incorporate it into all my publications as spiritual self-cultivation because it helps a person develop moral quality and character.

The warriors who carried the seeds of this spiritual culture sowed their spiritual practices throughout Asia and what is now called the Middle East, where the wise student Zoroaster developed them into a dualistic religion of black and white, bright and dark, good and evil. Heaven and hell became the mirrors of worldly confrontation. These concepts are all contained in the ancient theory of *T'ai Chi,* which encompasses the two spheres of *yin* and *yang* as interdependent rather than separate.

Religious worship originated from the development of cultivation of the inner light, which I describe as wakefulness in the subtle practice of Natural Meditation.

In Zoroastrian temples, a holy fire was maintained to symbolize the same inner light that was cultivated by the White Warriors. The God of Wisdom, Ah-Hu-Ra Ma-Zi-Da is the inner light that can be nurtured within a human being. This is the secret meaning of external worship.

In Syria, Mahavira Jina continued and developed the direction of Zoroaster. He also elaborated the war between white and black in his new religion, Manichaeism, which became widely accepted in the 4th century C.E. However, Mahavira Jina was persecuted by the King of Syria for his teachings because they conflicted with political and worldly benefit. He taught his followers to eat vegetables and refrain from sex in order to cultivate white light inside of the body, which conflicted with the king's worldly goals of having more soldiers and tax payers. The name Mahavira means light.

Later, the popularly worshipped Amitabha[9] was the personification of light in China. The Buddha of Great Sun (in Sanskrit, the Buddha of Universal Shining), the main deity of esoteric Buddhism in the Tung Dynasty (618-916 C.E.), also personified light.

In the 6th century C.E., Mohammed led people to follow the monotheism of the Jewish people and share the same ancestor, Abraham. It seems that the Jews and the Catholics neglected this opportunity for unification. Mohammed adopted a great deal of Christianity into his new religion,

---

[9]the Great Buddha, a man

but he also incorporated the concepts of a last judgment, an afterlife, etc., from Zoroastrianism. He called God Allah, which is similar to Ah Hu Ra, the divine one of Zoroaster.

A wise person can see through the fabric of external religion to the reality of all religions: the inner light or the light of the heart, which underlies all religious literature, art and ritual. As the enlightened ones declared: "Your heart is the real Buddha; the real Buddha is your own heart. There is no difference." All objects of worship are extensions of your own heart. A true student who knows such a deep fact will appreciate the ancient spiritual discipline of the Pure White Enterprise, the goal of which is personal improvement and higher evolution. You dare to be simple. You dare to be honest. You dare to stand upright by yourself, independent of any religious group.

With individual spiritual development, a person can realize that all religions express the "good will" of people because the source of all religions, if not too confused by their own external creations, is the inner light. It is important for all people to have good will toward one another, yet how do you know when your will is good? It depends on the level you have achieved through your own spiritual development. By practicing Natural Meditation, your clarity is not obstructed by any organized faith or technique. Spiritual development is based upon the fundamental discipline of the Pure White Enterprise as a whole system. A world of good will depends on the gain and achievement from the Pure White Enterprises of all of us.

As I mentioned in the Leading Song and at the end of the fifth section in Chapter 4, spiritual development is an important part of people's lives. There is no religion or science that can save the world. If they simply did no harm, that would be great progress.

Religion stubbornly holds onto what it believes, while science stubbornly insists upon "just the facts." The conflict between science and religion is based on a fundamental difference in the functions of a natural life: intellect vs.

feeling and affection. There is no need for conflict between the two, however. They can be used as counterchecks for each other to ensure the safety of science and reliability of religion.

The cultivation and study of natural spiritual reality goes far beyond general science or general religion. The subject and method of scientific research today is limited to that which is external. Religion, on the other hand, is not concerned with personal spiritual growth or achievement either. Religions tend to focus on spiritual phenomena that are associated with psychology and attempt to present the unpresentable subtle truth in a fossilizing way. Eventually, they obstruct the correct understanding of spiritual reality. No religion is the natural spirit itself. No serious spiritual student should wonder about or be confused by religious forms; one should work directly on their own essence. Direct spiritual learning is what I recommend.

A natural life has no need for any religion. A natural life is the religion from which all external religions developed. A serious spiritual student always remembers that one's personal spiritual achievement is what counts. Teachers who depend on the name of Jesus, Buddha, Mohammed or any past sages have not achieved their own spiritual independence. They are still at the stage of babies who crawl on the ground. How can they guide the future of the human race?

The world's troubles are not the fault of nature. So far, natural disaster has not been an overwhelming threat to human survival. The trouble of the world comes from people. Conflict will never end as long as people run after money, fame, influence and physical pleasure. Religion, science, politics, etc. are all useless unless spiritual development is valued and practiced among the most influential individuals. Otherwise, things will get worse before they get better. The people who need spiritual development most are leaders. You are one of them. I have given the direction for your spiritual enterprise through the self-study program in the *Golden Message*. In this investment, you will find no competition, for the benefit is invisible.

I hope you understand that before you start to teach, if you wish to do so, it is important to achieve spiritual independence directly from the unadorned truth and natural spiritual reality of life.

Real spiritual practice also has its limitations. Once I decided to teach some serviceable skills, which are not magic, but a service. However, I was warned against it by the condition of the modern generation which relies on police for its morality. Much useful knowledge and skill will only become forgotten treasures or lost memories if this trend is not reversed.

I recommend constancy, normalcy, orderliness, regularity and an ordinary life of decent fulfillment as the highest magic that can be performed. Nobody needs to become a magician. We all have sufficient natural power to fulfill a healthy, peaceful life.

About Hua-Ching Ni

The author, Hua-Ching Ni, feels that it is his responsibility to ensure that people receive his message clearly and correctly, thus, he puts his lectures and classes into book form. He does this for the clear purpose of universal spiritual unity.

It will be his great happiness to see the genuine progress of all people, all societies and nations as they become one big harmonious worldly community. This is the goal that inspires him to speak and write as one way of fulfilling his personal duty. The teachings he offers people come from his own growth and attainment.

Hua-Ching Ni began his spiritual pursuit when he was quite young. Although spiritual nature is innate, learning to express it suitably and usefully requires worldly experience and a lot of training. A hard life and hard work have made him deeper and stronger, and perhaps wiser. This is the case with all people who do not yield to the negative influences of life and the world. He does not intend to establish himself as a special individual, as do people in general spiritual society, but wishes to give service. He thinks that he is just one person living on the same plane of life with the rest of humanity.

He likes to be considered a friend rather than have a formal title. In this way he enjoys the natural spiritual response between himself and others who come together in extending the ageless natural spiritual truth to all.

He is a great traveller, and never tires of going to new places. His books have been printed in different languages, having been written at the side of his professional work as a natural healer – a fully trained Traditional Chinese Medical doctor. He understands that his world mission is to awaken people of both east and west, and he supports his friends and helpers as Mentors. All work together to fulfill the world spiritual mission of this time in human history.

Glossary

<u>Book of Changes:</u> See also *I Ching*. The legendary classic *Book of Changes* or the *I Ching* is recognized as the first written book of wisdom. Leaders and sages throughout history have consulted it as a trusted advisor which reveals the appropriate action in any circumstance.

<u>Chen Tuan, Master:</u> The "sleeping sage" who refreshed *T'ai Chi* philosophy, living circa 885-989 C.E. at the beginning of the Sung Dynasty.

<u>Chi</u> (also spelled *Qi* or *Ki*): *Chi* is the vitality or life energy of the universe and resides within each living being. In humans, it provides the power for our movements of body and mind, immune system, and all organ functions.

<u>Chi Kung</u> (also spelled *chi gong* or *qi gong*): Translated literally as energy work, energy exercise, or breathing exercise. A set of breathing, movement and/or visualization exercises for strengthening and balancing the *chi* or vital force, relaxing the mind, maintaining health and curing disease. It can be static (no movement) or dynamic (with movement). It is usually a single exercise or a small group of exercises practiced separately or together.

<u>Chuang Tzu:</u> A Taoist sage who lived around 275 B.C. and wrote an influential book called *Chuang Tzu*.

<u>Dao-In:</u> A series of *chi kung* type movements done sitting down traditionally used for conducting physical energy.

<u>Eight Treasures:</u> A form of *Dao-In*, a type of internal exercise or *chi kung* patterned after natural movements.

<u>I Ching:</u> A method of divination which uses the 64 hexagrams originated by Fu Shi. Information about the hexagrams was recorded in a book by the same name which is translated into English as *Book of Changes*.

<u>Integral Way (or the Way, or Tao):</u> The way of knowing, doing and being. The true spiritual achievement of the ancients. Realizing the *t'ai chi* principle of harmony and balance in life.

<u>Kou Hong, Master:</u> Also known in Chinese as Pao Poh Tzu or

Bao Boh Tzu. Living 283-262 C.E., during the Jing Dynasty. A balanced personality who provides a model of high spirituality.

Lao Tzu: Also expressed in Chinese as Lao Zi, Lao Tze , or Lao Tse. Achieved master who continued the teaching of natural truth. Author of the *Tao Teh Ching* and *Hua Hu Ching*. (Active around 571 B.C.E.)

Lu, Tung Ping, Master: Promoter of later school of spiritual swordsmanship which followed the moral discipline of Mo Tzu.

Meditation: A form of sitting, standing, or walking *chi kung* which develops centeredness to embrace all. Unites the mind with the body and gathers one's energy.

Sen (shen): Spirit; also the high or pure level of energy, which can be refined from *chi*.

T'ai Chi Movement: Also known in Chinese as *T'ai Chi Chuan* or *Tai Ji Quan*. Ancient Chinese exercise for harmonizing body, mind and spirit, whose connected movements somewhat resemble a graceful dance. Consists of many different *chi kung* movements put together sequentially and arranged with the principles given by the *Tao Teh Ching* and *I Ching*.

T'ai Chi Principle: The principle of alternation of opposites, also called the *Yin/Yang* Principle, the Universal Law, or the Law of *T'ai Chi*.

Tao: The invisible, Integral Way. Profound truth of life.

Tao Teh Ching: Also expressed in Chinese as *Dao Deh Jing*. An influential book written by Lao Tzu as an attempt to elucidate Tao, the subtle truth of life. Considered a classic, it is among the most widely translated and distributed books in the world.

Wu Wei: The principle of "doing nothing extra" or "inaction in action," "doing just enough," "non-doing," or "harmonious action."

Yin and Yang: Terms which describe opposites, the two ends of either pole, or duality. *Yang* relates to the male, outward, active, positive, fiery, energetic side of life or nature of a person. *Yin* relates to the female, inward, passive, negative, watery, cool, substantial side of life or nature of a person.

Teachings of the Universal Way by Hua-Ching Ni

NEW RELEASES

Spring Thunder: Awaken the Hibernating Power of Life - Humans need to be periodically awakened from a spiritual hibernation in which the awareness of life's reality is deeply forgotten. To awaken your deep inner life, this book offers the practice of Natural Meditation, the enlightening teachings of Yen Shi, and Master Ni's New Year Message. BSPRI 0-937064-77-7 PAPERBACK, 168 P $12.95

The Eight Treasures: Energy Enhancement Exercise - by Maoshing Ni, Ph. D. The Eight Treasures is an ancient system of energy enhancing movements based on the natural motion of the universe. It can be practiced by anyone at any fitness level, is non-impact, simple to do, and appropriate for all ages. It is recommended that this book be used with its companion videotape. BEIGH 0-937064-55-6 Paperback 208p $17.95

The Universal Path of Natural Life - The way to make your life enduring is to harmonize with the nature of the universe. By doing so, you expand beyond your limits to reach universal life. This book is the third in the series called *The Course for Total Health*. BUNIV 0-937064-76-9 PAPERBACK, 104P $9.50

Power of Positive Living How do you know if your spirit is healthy? You do not need to be around sickness to learn what health is. When you put aside the cultural and social confusion around you, you can rediscover your true self and restore your natural health. This is the second book of *The Course for Total Health*. BPOWE 0-937064-90-4 PAPERBACK 80P $8.50

The Gate to Infinity - People who have learned spiritually through years without real progress will be thoroughly guided by the important discourse in this book. Master Ni also explains Natural Meditation. Editors recommend that all serious spiritual students who wish to increase their spiritual potency read this one. BGATE 0-937064-68-8 PAPERBACK 208P $13.95

The Yellow Emperor's Classic of Medicine - by Maoshing Ni, Ph.D. The *Neijing* is one of the most important classics of Taoism, as well as the highest authority on traditional Chinese medicine. Written in the form of a discourse between Yellow Emperor and his ministers, this book contains a wealth of knowledge on holistic medicine and how human life can attune itself to receive natural support. BYELLO 1-57062-080-6 PAPERBACK 316P $16.00

Self-Reliance and Constructive Change - Natural spiritual reality is independent of concept. Thus dependence upon religious convention, cultural notions and political ideals must be given up to reach full spiritual potential. The Declaration of Spiritual Independence affirms spiritual self-authority and true wisdom as the highest attainments of life. This is the first book in *The Course for Total Health*. BSELF 0-937064-85-8 PAPERBACK 64P $7.00

Concourse of All Spiritual Paths - All religions, in spite of their surface difference, in their essence return to the great oneness. Hua-Ching Ni looks at what traditional religions offer us today and suggests how to go beyond differences to discover the depth of universal truth. BCONC 0-937064-61-0 PAPERBACK 184P $15.95.

PRACTICAL LIVING

The Key to Good Fortune: Refining Your Spirit - Straighten Your Way *(Tai Shan Kan Yin Pien)* and The Silent Way of Blessing *(Yin Chia Wen)* are the main guidance for a mature, healthy life. Spiritual improvement can be an integral part of realizing a Heavenly life on Earth. BKEYT 0-937064-39-4 PAPERBACK 144P $12.95

Harmony - The Art of Life - The emphasis in this book is on creating harmony within ourselves so that we can find it in relationships with other people and with our environment. BHARM 0-937064-37-8 PAPERBACK 208P $14.95

Ageless Counsel for Modern Life - Following the natural organization of the *I Ching*, Hua-Ching Ni has woven inspired commentaries to each of the 64 hexagrams. Taken alone, they display an inherent wisdom which is both personal and profound. BAGEL 0-937064-50-5 PAPERBACK 256P $15.95.

Strength From Movement: Mastering Chi - by Hua-Ching Ni, Daoshing Ni and Maoshing Ni. - *Chi*, the vital power of life, can be developed and cultivated within yourself to help support your healthy, happy life. This book gives the deep reality of different useful forms of *chi* exercise and which types are best for certain types of people. Includes samples of several popular exercises. BSTRE 0-937064-73-4 PAPERBACK WITH 42 PHOTOGRAPHS 256P $16.95.

8,000 Years of Wisdom, Volume I and II - This two-volume set contains a wealth of practical, down-to-earth advice given to students over a five-year period. Volume I includes 3 chapters on dietary guidance. Volume II devotes 7 chapters to sex and pregnancy topics. VOLUME I: BWIS1 0-937064-07-6 PAPERBACK 236P $12.50 • VOLUME II: BWIS2 0-937064-08-4 PAPERBACK 241P $12.50

The Time is Now for a Better Life and a Better World - What is the purpose of personal spiritual achievement if not to serve humanity by improving the quality of life for everyone? Hua-Ching Ni offers his vision of humanity's dilemma and what can be done about it. BTIME 0-937064-63-7 PAPERBACK 136P $10.95

Spiritual Messages from a Buffalo Rider, A Man of Tao - This book is a collection of talks from Hua-Ching Ni's world tour and offers valuable insights into the interaction between a compassionate spiritual teacher and his students from many countries around the world. BSPIR 0-937064-34-3 PAPERBACK 242P $12.95

Golden Message - by Daoshing and Maoshing Ni - This book is a distillation of the teachings of the Universal Way of Life as taught by the authors' father, Hua-Ching Ni. Included is a complete program of study for students and teachers of the Way. BGOLD 0-937064-36-x PAPERBACK 160P $11.95

Moonlight in the Dark Night - This book contains wisdom on how to control emotions, including how to manage love relationships so that they do not impede one's spiritual achievement. BMOON 0-937064-44-0 PAPERBACK 168P $12.95

SPIRITUAL DEVELOPMENT

Life and Teaching of Two Immortals, Volume 1: Kou Hong - A master who achieved spiritual ascendancy in 363 A.D., Kou Hong was an achieved master in the art of alchemy. His teachings apply the Universal Way to business, politics, emotions, human relationships, health and destiny. BLIF1 0-937064-47-5 PAPERBACK 176P $12.95.

Life and Teaching of Two Immortals, Volume 2: Chen Tuan - Chen Tuan was an achieved master who was famous for the foreknowledge he attained through deep study of the *I Ching* and for his unique method of "sleeping cultivation." This book also includes important details about the microcosmic meditation and mystical instructions from the "Mother of Li Mountain." BLIF2 0-937064-48-3 PAPERBACK 192P $12.95

The Way, the Truth and the Light - *now available in paperback!* - Presented in light, narrative form, this inspiring story unites Eastern and Western beliefs as it chronicles a Western prophet who journeys to the East in pursuit of further spiritual guidance. BLIGH1 0-937064-56-4 PAPERBACK 232P $14.95 • BLIGH2 0-937064-67-X HARDCOVER 232P $22.95

The Mystical Universal Mother - Hua-Ching Ni responds to the questions of his female students through the example of his mother and other historical and mythical women. He focuses on the feminine aspect of both sexes and on the natural relationship between men and women. BMYST 0-937064-45-9 PAPERBACK 240P $14.95

Eternal Light - Dedicated to Yo San Ni, a renowned healer and teacher, and father of Hua-Ching Ni. An intimate look at the lifestyle of a spiritually centered family. BETER 0-937064-38-6 PAPERBACK 208P $14.95

Quest of Soul - How to strengthen your soul, achieve spiritual liberation, and unite with the universal soul. A detailed discussion of the process of death is also included. BQUES 0-937064-26-2 PAPERBACK 152P $11.95

Nurture Your Spirits - Spirits are the foundation of our being. Hua-Ching Ni reveals the truth about "spirits" based on his personal cultivation and experience, so that you can nurture your own spirits. BNURT 0-937064-32-7 PAPERBACK 176P $12.95

Internal Alchemy: The Natural Way to Immortality - Ancient spiritually achieved ones used alchemical terminology metaphorically to disguise personal internal energy transformation. This book offers the prescriptions that help sublimate your energy. BALCH 0-937064-51-3 PAPERBACK 288P $15.95

Mysticism: Empowering the Spirit Within - "Fourteen Details for Immortal Medicine" is a chapter on meditation for women and men. Four other chapters are devoted to the study of 68 mystical diagrams, including the ones on Lao Tzu's tower. BMYST2 0-937064-46-7 PAPERBACK 200P $13.95

Internal Growth through Tao - In this volume, Hua-Ching Ni teaches about the more subtle, much deeper aspects of life. He also points out the confusion caused by some spiritual teachings and encourages students to cultivate internal growth. BINTE 0-937064-27-0 PAPERBACK 208P $13.95

Essence of Universal Spirituality - A review of world religions, revealing the harmony of their essence and helping readers enjoy the achievements of all religions without becoming confused by them. BESSE 0-937064-35-1 PAPERBACK 304P $19.95

Guide to Inner Light - Modern culture diverts our attention from our natural life being. Drawing inspiration from the experience of the ancient achieved ones, Hua-Ching Ni redirects modern people to their true source and to the meaning of life. BGUID 0-937064-30-0 PAPERBACK 192P $12.95

Stepping Stones for Spiritual Success - This volume contains practical and inspirational quotations from the traditional teachings of Tao. The societal values and personal virtues extolled here are relevant to any time or culture. BSTEP 0-937064-25-4 PAPERBACK 160P $12.95.

The Story of Two Kingdoms - The first part of this book is the metaphoric tale of the conflict between the Kingdoms of Light and Darkness. The second part details the steps to self-cleansing and self-confirmation. BSTOR 0-937064-24-6HARDCOVER 122P $14.50

The Gentle Path of Spiritual Progress - A companion volume to Messages of a Buffalo Rider. Hua-Ching Ni answers questions on contemporary psychology, sex, how to use the I Ching, and tells some fascinating spiritual legends! BGENT 0-937064-33-5 PAPERBACK 290P $12.95.

Footsteps of the Mystical Child - Profound examination of such issues as wisdom and spiritual evolution open new realms of understanding and personal growth. BFOOT 0-937064-11-4 PAPERBACK 166P $9.50

TIMELESS CLASSICS

The Complete Works of Lao Tzu - The *Tao Teh Ching* is one of the most widely translated and cherished works of literature. Its timeless wisdom provides a bridge to the subtle spiritual truth and aids harmonious and peaceful living. Plus the only authentic written translation of the *Hua Hu Ching*, a later work of Lao Tzu which was lost to the general public for a thousand years. BCOMP 0-937064-00-9 PAPERBACK 212P $13.95

The Book of Changes and the Unchanging Truth - Revised Edition - This version of the timeless classic *I Ching* is heralded as the standard for modern times. A unique presentation including profound illustrative commentary and details of the book's underlying natural science and philosophy from a world-renowned expert. BBOOK 0-937064-81-5 HARDCOVER 669P $35.00

Workbook for Spiritual Development - This is a practical, hands-on approach for those devoted to spiritual achievement. Diagrams show sitting postures, standing postures and even a sleeping cultivation. An entire section is devoted to ancient invocations. BWORK 0-937064-06-8 PAPERBACK 240P $14.95

The Esoteric Tao Teh Ching - This totally new edition offers instruction for studying the Tao Teh Ching and reveals the spiritual practices "hidden" in Lao Tzu's classic. These include in-depth techniques for advanced spiritual benefit. BESOT 0-937064-49-1 PAPERBACK 192P $13.95

The Way of Integral Life - The Universal Integral Way leads to a life of balance, health and harmony. This book includes practical suggestions for daily life, philosophical thought, esoteric insight and guidelines for those aspiring to help their lives and the world. BWAYS 0-937064-20-3 PAPERBACK 320P $14.00 • BWAYH 0-937064-21-1 HARDCOVER 320P $20.00.

Enlightenment: Mother of Spiritual Independence - The inspiring story and teachings of Hui Neng, the 6th Patriarch and father of Zen, highlight this volume. Intellectually unsophisticated, Hui Neng achieved himself to become a true spiritual revolutionary. BENLS 0-937064-19-X PAPERBACK 264P $12.50 • BENLH 0-937064-22-X HARDCOVER 264P $22.00.

Attaining Unlimited Life - Most scholars agree that Chuang Tzu produced some of the greatest literature in Chinese history. He also laid the foundation for the Universal Way. In this volume, Hua-Ching Ni draws upon his extensive training to rework the entire book of Chuang Tzu. BATTS 0-937064-18-1 PAPERBACK 467P $18.00; BATTH 0-937064-23-8 HARDCOVER $25.00

The Taoist Inner View of the Universe - This book offers a glimpse of the inner world and immortal realm known to achieved individuals and makes it understandable for students aspiring to a more complete life. BTAOI 0-937064-02-5 218P $14.95

Tao, the Subtle Universal Law - Thoughts and behavior evoke responses from the invisible net of universal energy. This book explains how self-discipline leads to harmony with the universal law. BTAOS 0-937064-01-7 PAPERBACK 208P $12.95

MUSIC AND MISCELLANEOUS

Colored Dust - Sung by Gaille. Poetry by Hua-Ching Ni. - The poetry of Hua-Ching Ni set to music creates a magical sense of transcendence through sound. 37 MINUTES ADUST CASSETTE $10.98, ADUST2 COMPACT DISC $15.95

Poster of Master Lu - Shown on cover of Workbook for Spiritual Development to be used in one's shrine. PMLTP 16" x 22" $10.95

POCKET BOOKLETS

Guide to Your Total Well-Being - Simple useful practices for self-development, aid for your spiritual growth and guidance for all aspects of life. Exercise, food, sex, emotional balancing, meditation. BWELL 0-937064-78-5 PAPERBACK 48P $4.00

Progress Along the Way: Life, Service and Realization - The guiding power of human life is the association between the developed mind and the achieved soul which contains love, rationality, conscience and everlasting value. BPROG 0-937-064-79-3 PAPERBACK 64P $4.00

The Light of All Stars Illuminates the Way - Through generations of searching, various achieved ones found the best application of the Way in their lives. This booklet contains their discovery. BSTAR 0-937064-80-7 48P $4.00

Less Stress, More Happiness - Helpful information for identifying and relieving stress in your life including useful techniques such as invocations, breathing and relaxation, meditation, exercise, nutrition and lifestyle balancing. BLESS 0-937064-55-06 48P $3.00

Integral Nutrition - Nutrition is an integral part of a healthy, natural life. Includes information on how to assess your basic body type, food preparation, energetic properties of food, nutrition and digestion. BNUTR 0-937064-84-X 32P $3.00

The Heavenly Way - Straighten Your Way (*Tai Shan Kan Yin Pien*) and The Silent Way of Blessing (*Yin Chia Wen*) are the main sources of inspiration for this booklet that sets the cornerstone for a mature, healthy life. BHEAV 0-937064-03-3 PAPERBACK 42P $2.50

HEALTH AND HEALING

Power of Natural Healing - This book is for anyone wanting to heal themselves or others. Methods include revitalization with acupuncture and herbs, *Tai Chi, Chi Kung (Chi Gong)*, sound, color, movement, visualization and meditation. BHEAL 0-937064-31-9 PAPERBACK 230P $14.95

Attune Your Body with *Dao-In* - The ancient Taoist predecessor to *Tai Chi Chuan*, these movements can be performed sitting and lying down to guide and refine your energy. Includes meditations and massage for a complete integral fitness program. To be used in conjunction with the video. BDAOI 0-937065-40-8 PAPERBACK WITH PHOTOGRAPHS 144P $14.95

101 Vegetarian Delights - by Lily Chuang and Cathy McNease - A lovely cookbook with recipes as tasty as they are healthy. Features multi-cultural recipes, appendices on Chinese herbs and edible flowers and a glossary of special foods. Over 40 illustrations. B101V 0-937064-13-0 PAPERBACK 176P $12.95

The Tao of Nutrition - by Maoshing Ni, Ph.D., with Cathy McNease, B.S., M.H. - Learn how to take control of your health with good eating. Over 100 common foods are discussed with their energetic properties and therapeutic functions listed. Food remedies for numerous common ailments are also presented. BNUTR 0-937064-66-1 PAPERBACK 214P $14.50

Chinese Vegetarian Delights - by Lily Chuang - An extraordinary collection of recipes based on principles of traditional Chinese nutrition. Meat, sugar, dairy products and fried foods are excluded. BCHIV 0-937064-13-0 PAPERBACK 104P $7.50

Chinese Herbology Made Easy - by Maoshing Ni, Ph.D. - This text provides an overview of Oriental medical theory, in-depth descriptions of each herb category, over 300 black and white photographs, extensive tables of individual herbs for easy reference and an index of pharmaceutical names. BCHIH 0-937064-12-2 PAPERBACK 202P $14.50

Crane Style Chi Gong Book - By Daoshing Ni, Ph.D. - Standing meditative exercises practiced for healing. Combines breathing techniques, movement, and mental imagery to guide the smooth flow of energy. To be used with or without the videotape. BCRAN 0-937064-10-6 SPIRAL-BOUND 55P $10.95

VIDEOTAPES

Natural Living and the Universal Way (VHS) - New! - Interview of Hua-Ching Ni in the show "Asian-American Focus" hosted by Lily Chu. Dialogue on common issues of everyday life and practical wisdom. VINTE VHS VIDEO 30 MINUTES $15.95

Movement Arts for Emotional Health (VHS) -New! - Interview of Hua-Ching Ni in the show "Asian-American Focus" hosted by Lily Chu. Dialogue on emotional health and energy exercise that are fundamental to health and well-being. VMOVE VHS VIDEO 30 MINUTES $15.95

Attune Your Body with Dao-In (VHS) - by Master Hua-Ching Ni. - The ancient Taoist predecessor to Tai Chi Chuan. Performed sitting and lying down, these moves unblock, guide and refine energy. Includes meditations and massage for a complete integral fitness program. VDAOI VHS VIDEO 60 MINUTES $39.95

Tai Chi Ch'uan: An Appreciation (VHS) - by Hua-Ching Ni. - "Gentle Path," "Sky Journey" and "Infinite Expansion" are three esoteric styles handed down by highly achieved masters and are shown in an uninterrupted format. Not an instructional video. VAPPR VHS VIDEO 30 MINUTES $24.95

Self-Healing Chi Gong (VHS Video) - Strengthen your own self-healing powers. These effective mind-body exercises strengthen and balance each of your five major organ systems. Two hours of practical demonstrations and information lectures. VSHCG VHS VIDEO 120 MINUTES $39.95

Crane Style Chi Gong (VHS) - by Dr. Daoshing Ni, Ph.D. - These ancient exercises are practiced for healing purposes. They integrate movement, mental imagery and breathing techniques. To be used with the book. VCRAN VHS VIDEO 120 MINUTES $39.95

Taoist Eight Treasures (VHS) - By Maoshing Ni, Ph.D. - Unique to the Ni family, these 32 exercises open and refine the energy flow and strengthen one's vitality. Combines stretching, toning and energy conducting with deep breathing Book also available. VEIGH VHS VIDEO 105 MINUTES $39.95

***T'ai Chi Ch'uan* I & II (VHS)** - By Maoshing Ni, Ph.D. - This style, called the style of Harmony, is a distillation of the Yang, Chen and Wu styles. It integrates physical movement with internal energy and helps promote longevity and self-cultivation. VTAI1 VHS VIDEO PART 1 60 MINUTES $39.95 • VTAI2 VHS VIDEO PART 2 60 MINUTES $39.95

AUDIO CASSETTES

Invocations for Health, Longevity and Healing a Broken Heart - By Maoshing Ni, Ph.D. - "Thinking is louder than thunder." This cassette guides you through a series of invocations to channel and conduct your own healing energy and vital force. AINVO AUDIO 30 MINUTES $9.95

Stress Release with Chi Gong - By Maoshing Ni, Ph.D. - This audio cassette guides you through simple breathing techniques that enable you to release stress and tension that are a common cause of illness today. ACHIS AUDIO 30 MINUTES $9.95

Pain Management with Chi Gong - By Maoshing Ni, Ph.D. - Using visualization and deep-breathing techniques, this cassette offers methods for overcoming pain by invigorating your energy flow and unblocking obstructions that cause pain. ACHIP AUDIO 30 MINUTES $9.95

Tao Teh Ching Cassette Tapes - The classic work of Lao Tzu in this two-cassette set is a companion to the book translated by Hua-Ching Ni. Professionally recorded and read by Robert Rudelson. ATAOT 120 MINUTES $12.95

BOOKS IN SPANISH
Tao Teh Ching - En Español. BSPAN 0-937064-92-0 PAPERBACK 112 P $8.95

Order Form

SEVEN STAR
COMMUNICATIONS

name _____

street address _____

city _____ state _____ zip _____

country _____ best time to call _____

phone (day) _____ (evening) _____

Credit Card Information (VISA or MasterCard Only)

Credit Card No. _____

Exp. Date _____

Signature _____

Quantity	Price	Title	5 Letter Code	Total

Sub total	
Sales tax (CA residents only, 8.25%)	
Shipping (see left)	
Total Amount Enclosed	

Mail this form with payment
(US funds only) to:
SevenStar Communications
1314 Second Street
Santa Monica, CA 90401 USA

Credit Card Orders:
call **1-800-578-9526**
or fax **310-917-2267**

E-Mail Orders:
taostar@ix.netcom.com

Other Inquiries
1-310-576-1901

Shipping Charges

Number of items	Domestic		International			
	UPS Ground	4th Class Book Rate US Mail	Surface US Mail	Air [2] Printed Matter US Mail	Air Parcel Rate US Mail	UPS Int'l Air
First item [1]	4.50	2.00	2.50	7.50	12.00	46.00
Each Additional item	0.50	0.50	1.00	5.00[3]	6.00	6.00

NOTES
1 BOOK OF CHANGES (I CHING) because of weight, counts as 3 items, all other books count as one item each.
2 US Mail Air Printed Matter Table to be used for European destination only. All others use Parcel rate.
3 Limit of 4 items only for this service.

DELIVERY TIMES
UPS Ground: 7-10 days, Insured
4th Class Book Rate USmail: 5-8 week, Uninsured
Surface US mail (Overseas): 6-9 weeks, Uninsured
Air Printed Matter USmail (Overseas): 2-4 weeks, Uninsured
Air Parcel Rate USmail: 2-4 weeks, Insured
UPS International Air: 4 days, Insured

Spiritual Study and Teaching
Through the College of Tao

The College of Tao (COT) and the Union of Tao and Man were formally established in California in the 1970's, yet this tradition is a very broad spiritual culture containing centuries of human spiritual growth. Its central goal is to offer healthy spiritual education to all people to help individuals develop themselves for a spiritually developed world. This time-tested "school without walls" values the spiritual development of each individual self and passes down its guidance and experience.

COT does not use an institution with a building. Human society is its classroom. Your own life and service are the class you attend; thus students learn from their lives and from studying the guidance of the Universal Way.

Any interested individual is welcome to join and learn for oneself. The Self-Study Program that is based on Master Ni's books and videotapes gives people who wish to study on their own, or are too far from a teacher, an opportunity to study the Universal Way. The outline for the Self-Study Program is given in the book *The Golden Message*. If you choose, a Correspondence Course is also available.

A Mentor is any individual who is spiritually self-responsible and who is a model of a healthy and complete life. A Mentor may serve as a teacher for general society and people with a preliminary interest in spiritual development. To be certified to teach, a Mentor must first register with the Universal Society of the Integral Way (USIW) and follow the Mentor Service Handbook, which was written by Mentors. It is recommended that all prospective Mentors use the Correspondence Course or self-study program to educate themselves, but they may also learn directly from other Mentors. COT offers special seminars taught only to Mentors.

If you are interested in the Integral Way of Life Correspondence Course, please write: College of Tao, PO Box 1222, El Prado, NM 87529 USA.

- -

If you would like more information about the USIW and classes in your area, please send the following form to: USIW, PO Box 28993, Atlanta, GA 30358-0993 USA

☐   I wish to be put on the mailing list of the USIW to be notified of educational activities.

☐   I wish to receive a list of Registered Mentors teaching in my area or country.

☐   I am interested in joining/forming a study group in my area.

☐   I am interested in becoming a member or Mentor of the USIW.

Name:_____

Address:_____

City:_____State:_____Zip:_____

Country:_____

Phone, Fax and/or E-mail_____

Herbs Used by Ancient Masters

The pursuit of everlasting youth or immortality throughout human history is an innate human desire. Long ago, Chinese esoteric Taoists went to the high mountains to contemplate nature, strengthen their bodies, empower their minds and develop their spirits. From their studies and cultivation, they gave China alchemy and chemistry, herbology and acupuncture, the I Ching, astrology, martial arts and T'ai Chi Ch'uan, Chi Gong and many other useful kinds of knowledge.

Most important, they handed down in secrecy methods for attaining longevity and spiritual immortality. There were different levels of approach; one was to use a collection of food herb formulas available only to highly achieved Taoist masters. They used these food herbs to increase energy and heighten vitality. This treasured collection of herbal formulas remained within the Ni family for centuries.

Now, through Traditions of Tao, the Ni family makes these foods available for you to use to assist the foundation of your own positive development. It is only with a strong foundation that expected results are produced from diligent cultivation.

As a further benefit, in concert with the Taoist principle of self-sufficiency, Traditions of Tao offers the food herbs along with SevenStar Communication's publications in a distribution opportunity for anyone serious about financial independence.

Send to: Traditions of Tao
1314 Second Street #200
Santa Monica, CA 90401

Please send me a Traditions of Tao brochure.

Name _____

Address_____

City_____State_____Zip_____

Phone (day)_____(evening)_____

Yo San University of Traditional Chinese Medicine

"Not just a medical career, but a life-time commitment to raising one's spiritual standard."

Thank you for your support and interest in our publications and services. It is by your patronage that we continue to offer you the practical knowledge and wisdom from this venerable Taoist tradition.

Because of your sustained interest in natural health, in January 1989 we formed Yo San University of Traditional Chinese Medicine, a non-profit educational institution under the direction of founder Master Ni, Hua-Ching. Yo San University is the continuation of 38 generations of Ni family practitioners who handed down their knowledge and wisdom. Its purpose is to train and graduate practitioners of the highest caliber in Traditional Chinese Medicine, which includes acupuncture, herbology and spiritual development.

We view Traditional Chinese Medicine as the application of spiritual development. Its foundation is the spiritual capability to know life, diagnose a person's problem and cure it. We teach students how to care for themselves and others, emphasizing the integration of traditional knowledge and modern science. Yo San University offers a complete accredited Master's degree program approved by the California State Department of Education that provides an excellent education in Traditional Chinese Medicine and meets all requirements for state licensure. Federal financial aid and scholarships are available, and we accept students from all countries.

We invite you to inquire into our university for a creative and rewarding career as a holistic physician. Classes are also open to persons interested in self-enrichment. For more information, please fill out the form below and send it to:

Yo San University of Traditional Chinese Medicine
1314 Second Street
Santa Monica, CA 90401 U.S.A.

❑ Please send me information on the Masters degree program in Traditional Chinese Medicine.

❑ Please send me information on the massage certificate program.

❑ Please send me information on health workshops and seminars.

❑ Please send me information on continuing education for acupuncturists and health professionals.

Name _____

Address _____

City _____ *State* _____ *Zip* _____

Phone (day) _____ *(evening)* _____

Index